Young Professional's
Guide to the

WORKING
WORLD

The
Young Professional's
Guide to the
WORKING
WORLD

Savvy Strategies to
Get in, Get Ahead,
and Rise to the Top

Foreword by Marshall Goldsmith

New York Times best-selling author of
What Got You Here Won't Get You There

Aaron McDaniel

CAREER
PRESS
Pompton Plains, N.J.

THE YOUNG PROFESSIONAL'S GUIDE TO THE WORKING WORLD
EDITED AND TYPESET BY KARA KUMPEL
Cover design by Howard Grossman/12E Design
Printed in the U.S.A.

To order this title, please call toll-free 1-800-CAREER-1 (NJ and Canada: 201-848-0310) to order using VISA or MasterCard, or for further information on books from Career Press.

The Career Press, Inc.
220 West Parkway, Unit 12
Pompton Plains, NJ 07444
www.careerpress.com

Library of Congress Cataloging-in-Publication Data

McDaniel, Aaron.
    The young professional's guide to the working world : savvy strategies to get in, get ahead, and rise to the top / by Aaron McDaniel ; foreword by Marshall Goldsmith.
        p. cm.
    Includes index.
    ISBN 978-1-60163-242-5 -- ISBN 978-1-60163-556-3 (ebook)
    1. Success in business. 2. Career development. 3. Professions. I. Title.
HF5386.M4743 2013
650.1--dc23

2012023253

To my mom, Dawn, who stretched the bounds of creativity to teach me the necessity of integrity, the power of believing in myself, the benefit of never giving up, and the importance of always giving things a shot before labeling a situation impossible.

To my dad, Jerry, who groomed me to be a business leader from a young age, having me build budgets and schedules, always warning that one day I would have a boss; who assured me I would eventually reach the top, made me eliminate the word *can't* from my vocabulary, and taught me that *to know and not to do is not to know.*

This book is dedicated to you both. I love you.

Acknowledgments

So many people helped make this great concept a reality.

To Zach Romano, my agent: Thank you for believing in me and singling out this idea among the stacks and stacks you come across every day. It seems as though it all moved so fast. Once we connected, you jumped into action, and before I could blink we were already down the path to finding the right home for the book. I also want to thank Carole Jelen and the rest of the team at Waterside Productions for helping throughout the entire process.

To the entire team at Career Press: You have been an absolute pleasure to work with. Kirsten Dalley, Gina Talucci, and Kara Kumpel, my editors, I am grateful for how you have always been there to answer my questions and have been flexible in getting everything ready for print. Jeff Piasky, I LOVE the silhouette design idea; it definitely makes the cover pop. Thanks to Laurie Kelly-Pye and the Newman Communications team for working hard to get the word out about the book. Awesome job everyone!

A big shout-out to my manuscript readers! Leona Ma, Jonathan Siegel, Suzanne O'Brien, and Glenn Devore, thank you so much for taking the time to comb through the mistakes of my drafts to find ways to sharpen my message and make the book more useful for the readers. I am indebted to each of you for how you challenged me to make my book even better. It definitely shows in the finished product.

Thanks to Marco Cozzi, Sarah Tran, Pedro Noyola, Juan Contreras, Shweta Sharma, Jeff Haskins, Kate Calligaro, and Glenn Devore for your help on the Quick Tips. Hopefully the success each of you has found in your careers will rub off on the readers.

My gratitude goes out to Nii Mensah, Virginia de Freitas Battersby, and others for lending me the perfect stories to help make my key points sink in.

To Paul Benjamin: Thanks for the support, encouragement, and for being the best photographer in the world. Your pictures (and vision) are amazing.

Special thanks to Chimmy Lee. Chimmy, your graphics are always tops. You really brought the Career Blueprint idea to life in a way I never could have.

Marshall Goldsmith: Your foreword really sets the tone for the book and your tireless and selfless effort to help others be the best leaders they can be is nothing short of inspiring. I am honored that you were willing to contribute to this project.

Having solid mentors is one of the most important ingredients for a successful career. This book would not have happened without the support and guidance of Alexandra Levit, Dan Schwabel, and (without even knowing it) Michael Larsen. You all pushed me to make this idea a reality and pulled back the veil on what it takes to be a successful author. To Chris Sambar: thanks for teaching me to take my career to the next level, from how to dress professionally to how to get people to support your ideas. And to my very first mentor, my cousin Sean Sunday: Sean, you helped turn me from a scrappy little kid into a stand-up guy. I love ya BOC.

Joan Massola: You are a delight in every sense of the word. From allowing me to bounce ideas off of you to offering guidance on how to make this book exactly what young professionals need to hear—all of it is much appreciated. You are pretty awesome at giving career advice too!

Rich Heffernan: Thank you for having faith that I would be a good intern-turned-manager. Your confidence in me has led to an amazing career so far. I am so glad I didn't hit "Send" on that e-mail to you.

Chris Garner: I am indebted to you for challenging me to be "not *just*." The first time we met may have been only a few moments but it had a huge impact on me. Plus it makes for one heck of a story!

I want to acknowledge all the **STAR**s and **DOPE**s out there. You all have helped me learn many incredibly valuable lessons.

Finally (and most importantly), Mom and Dad, I want to express my appreciation to you. You taught me from a young age almost every one of the lessons in this book. Through twists of fate and amazing parenting alike, you engrained these characteristics into me. I strive to make you proud of me in everything I do. Words can't express the love I have for each of you.

Thank you!

Contents

Part V: Bringing It All Together

Foreword
by Marshall Goldsmith

Aaron McDaniel's *The Young Professional's Guide to the Working World: Savvy Strategies to Get In, Get Ahead, and Rise to the Top* is a significant work, as its focus is on guiding young professionals—millennials—in the first years of their corporate careers. In the field of leadership, there aren't many books focused on the traits and skills this audience needs in order to face today's corporate challenges and succeed in the current business environment. This books is highly valuable for this audience.

One of the most difficult challenges these young professionals face is an environment of constant and rapid change for which there is no established model of leadership. Although executive management models of the past provide some guidance for the leadership models of the future, in today's complex and ever-changing worldwide business environment, no specific, established model will fit the broad range of situations these young leaders will encounter.

That's why this book is so useful to young professionals today. It provides insights on qualities and traits that are becoming increasingly important to have if these millennials are going to succeed. Aaron is a millennial himself, and so has experience, knowledge, and personal learnings to share that many of us who were brought up in different times may not.

Personally, I believe that young professionals today have to demonstrate an entrepreneurial spirit if they are going to succeed in today's job market. They have to create opportunities where there might not seem to be one. It's not easy. We can't all be entrepreneurial in terms of how we approach our careers. Yet, there are things that we can do; here are a few suggestions.

- ✶ **Love what you do.** Years of hard work (which generally precedes success) don't seem so hard if you are doing what you love.

- ✶ **Be curious.** Make notes about potential opportunities, and then follow up on them.

- ✶ **Find your own market niche.** In the same way that successful entrepreneurs provide innovative solutions to market opportunities, you can work to develop a special competency that differentiates you from everyone else.

- ✶ **Become a world expert.** Pick a reasonably narrow area of specialization, focus on it, and learn as much as you can. You will start to accumulate serious knowledge within a few years. Although you can never become the world authority on everything, you can definitely become a world authority on one thing.

- ✶ **Learn from the best.** Ask yourself, *Who do I want to be like in 10 years?* Or, *Who are the world's experts in fields that are related to my desired area of expertise?* Learn from these people's lives. You may be surprised. Some may even go out of their way to help you.

- ✶ **Do your homework.** Although the role models you look up to may be willing to help you, respect the fact that they are very busy people. Their time is valuable. Study their history, read their bios or books, and learn about them and their work before you ask them to invest their very limited time in helping you.

* **Build your own brand.** Peter Drucker once told me that companies should be able to "put their mission statement on a T-shirt." The same can be true for individuals. What is your mission statement?

* **Pay the price.** It is possible that you may just get lucky and become incredibly successful without having to work very hard. Don't count on it. Successful people work hard.

I hope these suggestions are useful for you or young people you are striving to help. And, if used in combination with Aaron's ideas about taking ownership of your careers and building a strong career foundation, you will be in very good shape to become a successful young professional of the highest caliber.

I wish you much success for a bright, productive future!

Life is good.

Marshall Goldsmith

America's Preeminent Executive Coach (*Fast Company*),
Most Influential Leadership Thinker in the World
(*Harvard Business Review*), and million-selling
author/editor of 32 books, including *New York Times* best-sellers
MOJO and *What Got You Here Won't Get You There*

PART I

Starting Prep and Groundwork

CHAPTER 1

The Working World: No More Trophies for Participation

Whoever ceases to be a student has never been a student.
—George Iles

The only source of knowledge is experience.
—Albert Einstein

I was three months into my first job out of college and I was facing the event that each year strikes fear into the hearts of employees across the country. It was time for my first performance review.

Whereas many people are scared of having to face their boss and get (often critical) feedback about how they do their jobs, I, on the other hand, was excited.

Even though I had only been in my position for a short time, I felt I really had a handle on what I was doing. I had made an effort not to bother my boss with a laundry list of silly questions. Instead I relied on my peers and others in the office to teach me the systems I needed to use and the processes I needed to follow to fulfill my job responsibilities. I felt as though I was on the road to quickly mastering everything.

As I walked into her office I was expecting fireworks. I envisioned my boss talking about how all the work I had done was above and beyond what she expected. She would follow up by offering me a sizable raise, letting me know I was on the fast track to a promotion.

I sat down, and she began to go through my review. The first words that cut through the shuffling of chairs and paper were wildly different from what I expected: "Aaron, I'm just not sure that you really 'get it,'" she stated, followed by a long pause. "You appear to be a sharp young person but I rarely receive any feedback or questions from you, so I am not sure you really even understand how to do your job."

I was stunned. Her words still sting today.

In that moment, it become abundantly clear that despite all the time and effort I spent learning my job and working to impress my boss, I had committed one of the deadly sins that many of us commit when starting our careers: I failed to take the time to understand my boss. I didn't make an effort to connect with her and learn how she preferred to communicate and be communicated to.

My response to her statement, which escapes me because I am sure it was a mumbled mess of excuses, could not undo the damage I had done.

This was the first situation in my young career in which I realized beyond a shadow of a doubt that ***SCHOOL DOES NOT PREPARE YOU FOR YOUR CAREER.***

There is no course offered in college that teaches you how to interact with an executive asking you to complete a project. There is no textbook that outlines the steps you need to take to build a strong reputation and earn a solid promotion. Some of us come from backgrounds such that our family members didn't teach us about the corporate world because they had no corporate experience themselves. Some clubs and extracurricular activities may have taught us applicable skills, but we have almost no reference points to know how to be successful in the workplace.

Corporate leaders realize that we are different from previous generations. They see millennials (or "Gen Yers," or whatever they want to call us), as more than just texting, tweeting, Facebooking young employees; they see us as the future of their businesses. Because of this, corporations are finding ways to adapt for us. They are leveraging social media to recruit and are testing out new work models that appeal to our generation.

Corporate culture shifts are a great first step, but corporate planning only addresses half of the issue at hand. Many words have been associated with corporations, but the words *agile* and *quick* are not often among them. Change within companies takes time. Companies are not going to transform into familiar places for millennials to grow and thrive.

What's more notable is that a gigantic gap exists in the corporate world today. Corporate leaders are not dedicating enough time and resources to teach young professionals as individuals how to be successful in the current corporate world. Whereas many companies have comprehensive orientation conferences and assign mentors to new employees, most do not give each young professional the tools needed to understand how to maneuver complex corporate environments.

This leaves most of us with one option: to figure it out on our own.

It has been said that you never truly learn a lesson until you experience it yourself, but there is a better way. Enter *The Young Professional's Guide to the Working World*. This book contains lessons (six years in the making) from my career. By successfully applying the advice you are about to read you will be ahead of your peers, no matter how many years of work experience you may already have.

Because there aren't any courses on how to build a successful career, it is important to understand what the corporate world is and what it is not. Here are some of the expectations I had entering the corporate world that were completely false:

- ☆ **You will get a raise every year.** When the economy is bad companies use excess cash for things like keeping the lights on and retaining customers.

- ☆ **The higher your performance rating, the higher the raise.** Politics are also part of the equation. You don't always get what you think you *deserve*.

- ☆ **If you are a top performer you will always get your way.** More humbling stories to come.

- ☆ **You are smarter than everyone else.** Good companies tend to hire intelligent people, and as you make your way up the corporate ladder the people get smarter and savvier. Plus, these corporate leaders already have one more thing than we do: experience.

- ☆ **You can behave at work just as you did at college.** Many of us understand that this is false, but sometimes we make mistakes. (Think about company events that involve alcohol.)

- ☆ **You will be rewarded for being loyal to your company.** With such high pressure to meet quarterly earnings estimates and aggressive goals, corporations can make taking care of their people an afterthought. Dollars and cents trump people.

- ☆ **All of your coworkers will like and support you.** There will be people who won't like you. It may be because you are better at your job than they are. It may be because of a rumor someone made up about you, or it may even be because they think you looked at them weird once. No matter how nice you are, it will happen.

Now that we've proved some of my grandiose visions (and maybe some of yours) wrong, let's talk about some brutal truths about the working world that I learned the hard way.

6 things I wish I knew about companies before I started my career:

1. **Promotions don't come around often.** I had thought that as long as I was good at doing my job then I would be on the path to moving up to the next level. I also had this idea that it would happen fast. If you want to be CEO of a company, start your own. Or plan on taking 20-plus years to reach that level at a large corporation.

2. **Jumping around from company to company does not look good.** Working for four different companies in your first five years of work experience is a bad thing. Many friends and colleagues have taught me this lesson. A diverse set of entry-level experiences can be good, but if you start to show yourself as someone who jumps from place to place it will seem as though either (a) you have no idea what you want to do in your career (which may be true, but you don't need to let others know this), or (b) you lack resiliency and follow-through, and therefore would not be a good hire.

3. **You often won't have control of your own career.** This one was hard to swallow. I have found that the way to move up within a company (especially a big one) is to say yes when the higher-ups tell you to take on a new position or move to a new place. If you say no two or more times, they will stop asking and will find someone else who will say yes (which could potentially stall your career).

4. **It's not personal; it's just business.** People *are* important to companies, but the financial bottom line supersedes the individual.

5. **Your reputation alone won't carry your career.** Most of us have heard the phrase *What have you done for me lately?* A strong reputation is an important thing to develop, but people often think of you according to your latest accomplishment or how well you did in your most recent role.

6. **Your boss cares more about his or her career than yours.** I have been fortunate enough to work for some amazing bosses who have given me many opportunities and a great deal

of exposure. At the same time, don't forget that your bosses' and their families well-being will always come before yours.

Despite the dreary picture, there is still hope.

Although we don't always have control over our careers, **we need to take ownership of our career path**. We can seek mentors and work on being a constant learner (a mentor of mine calls this continually "sharpening your sword"). We can develop new skills and proactively seek challenging career opportunities that will stretch us to perform at a higher level.

You are already taking the first step in "sharpening your sword" by reading this book. A good second step is to leverage the peer mentorship and other resources available at TheSparkSource.com, where you can interact with other young professionals and learn key advice from experts in the field.

Here's a reminder of why you should read on: ***SCHOOL DOES NOT PREPARE YOU FOR YOUR CAREER.***

As you begin your career and start building a foundation to support the next 40 years of work you have two options: (1) take the time now to learn best practices and avoid common pitfalls, or (2) learn the hard way by making your own mistakes. By nature, we learn lessons through personal experience. Although this is one of the most effective ways to learn, I encourage you to learn from *my* mistakes and the mistakes of others instead. Mistakes can be helpful, but also painful. I want each of you to be successful in your careers while keeping career-limiting mistakes to a minimum. This book is not just for recent graduates. Understanding the principles in this book can help you take your career to the next level even if you have a few years of experience. These lessons become even more real and relatable when you have more career experience.

Why me?

It is common to hear success stories. The media likes to grab hold of tales such as Mark Zuckerberg's. However, it is important to understand that these situations are one in a billion. Whereas these stories can be inspiring and educational, it is hard for us to connect with them, and odds are most of us will never be in a situation in which we start a $100 billion company.

I believe it is more useful to focus on practical advice that is truly applicable to each of us; not just in extraordinary circumstances, but in our everyday lives. The advice I give is not based on some miraculous story. I am not special by any means. I did not come from a highly educated or wealthy family. In fact, we were coupon-cutters long before Groupon made using a coupon seem cool. I work hard (as do most of you), and I am ambitious about the things I am passionate about (also just as most of you). I learned as I went along.

There isn't a complicated formula I used to reach the level I have attained. On the contrary, my path has been shaped by two things:

1. I know that I am a leader. I understood early on that I can be a leader regardless of the situation or the task I am given. Being a leader does not always mean taking all the glory and being in the limelight. Being a leader means contributing my best effort to the team I am on and challenging myself to go to the next level.

2. I identified and began to develop the 25 attributes outlined in this book. Developing these characteristics takes time and is a continuous process that you need to consistently work at, so don't get intimidated and think that you need to master all 25 of these immediately.

Let me offer you background on what the ideas in this book have helped me accomplish while still in my 20's. I have:

* ★ Become one of the youngest people ever to serve as regional vice president at AT&T.

* ★ Managed more than 100 direct reports at different times (sometimes 15 at once).

* ★ Managed entire organizations as large as 60 people (10 of whom were area manager direct reports, with 50 people reporting to those 10).

* ★ Gained strong experience in marketing, sales, operations, strategy, customer service, and business development, each year receiving *exceeds expectations* on my annual performance reviews (except, of course, for that first review).

- ★ Been honored with being part of AT&T's Diamond Club, awarded to the top 1 percent of sales leaders worldwide.

- ★ Cofounded, built, and sold multiple businesses (including a portable beer-pong table company and a mobile application development company).

- ★ Taught a student-led course on leadership and organizational dynamics at the UC Berkeley Undergraduate Haas School of Business.

- ★ Created a nonprofit organization to fight for equality

- ★ Volunteered for education-related initiatives including the Full Circle Fund, Junior Achievement, and Big Brothers Big Sisters.

- ★ Literally earned the "corner office" while everyone else was stuck in cubeland.

- ★ Visited more than 33 countries (I am passionate about traveling).

I am proud of my accomplishments and I want to help you reach your career goals, too.

What will you get out of reading this book?

To take a lesson from my college marketing course, let me articulate to you, my customer, the WIIFM—*What's in it for me?*

By reading the 25 attributes of a successful young professional outlined in this book and by leveraging the resources and mentoring available on the Spark Source Website (*http://TheSparkSource.com*) you will:

- ★ Learn the 25 key characteristics to incorporate into your tool belt that will lead to more career success.

- ★ Gain valuable lessons based on corporate experience from real situations so you can put the advice provided into practical context, instead of just theory.

- ★ Utilize a structured framework to build and execute your own career plan.

- ★ Connect with other young professionals who offer support and encouragement as you conquer challenges at work.

I have found that many business books are repetitive, reiterating the same points over and over again. I have taken a different approach. As you read you will see that I generally get to the point and reinforce important advice with short, easy-to-understand stories. This allows you to learn more, faster.

Similar to most millennials, I have a short attention span. You'll find that the chapters are short and easy to get through. Plus, there are additional resources available online (as that is where we go to learn most things anyway).

In each of the following chapters, you will find the following:

✴ **What to Expect.** At the beginning of each chapter you will find a short summary of the main point of the chapter. This will give you a key takeaway and a basis for the examples referenced.

✴ **Quick Tips.** Small pieces of simple advice can often make a big difference. Sprinkled throughout the book you will find good-to-know tips.

✴ **Explore Online.** The Spark Source experience goes beyond the pages of this book to an ever-growing online community that reinvents career mentorship. References to items on TheSparkSource.com can be found under the Resources section of the site.

✴ **The STAR vs. The DOPE.** At the end of each chapter there is a recap contrasting the DOPE and the STAR as it relates to the topic discussed (The STAR and The DOPE are outlined in Chapter 2).

Our generation has also been called the "trophy generation." Although it is my least favorite of the labels attributed to us, there is some truth to it: We are used to being recognized and rewarded for just participating in something. I have a box full of certificates, ribbons, and, yes, trophies, just for being on a sports team, being a member of an organization, and for having good attendance at school. This is not the way of the corporate world.

The corporate world is a tough place. You will need to survive shark-infested waters. Dodge the perils of organizational change. Create constant positive results. It is best not to do it alone. Find mentors wherever you can, from experts to peers to leveraging resources available to you through your company and online.

The harsh reality is that in the corporate world there are no trophies or special recognition for participation. Doing your job is the baseline. You will need to deliver above and beyond what is expected. Get used to it. Oh, and welcome to the real world.

Yesterday is gone. Tomorrow has yet to come. We have only today. Let's begin.

—Mother Theresa

Chapter 2

Don't Be the DOPE: The Successful Young Professional's Mindset

What to Expect: This chapter outlines the foundation for a concept and persona referenced throughout the book, the Successful Young Professional (or **STAR**). What makes her/him successful? What does she/he do to build a strong foundation for a successful career? What mistakes does she/he avoid? This chapter addresses these questions and will also introduce you to the opposite of the **STAR**, the **DOPE**.

If you go to work on your goals, your goals will go to work on you. If you go to work on your plan, your plan will go to work on you. Whatever good things we build end up building us.

—Jim Rohn

Building almost anything takes focus and the ability to think things through, from building a multi-national company to a bookcase from IKEA. Take architect Henry Cobb, designer of the John Hancock Tower, as an example.

The John Hancock Tower soars above the streets of Boston and defines the city's skyline with its monolithic simplicity and reflective glass façade. Designed by Cobb and completed in 1976, this 60-story skyscraper received critical acclaim, including being awarded the National Honor Award from the American Institute of Architects. Having seen it in person when visiting Boston (my best friend actually worked in the building), I saw firsthand how sleek and triumphant it looks. Soon after completion, however, problems started to surface.

The soil of Boston's Back Bay neighborhood could not support the weight of the structure (including the 10,344 glass window panes, each weighing about 500 pounds) and high winds often afflicted those on the highest floors with motion sickness. Then the building literally began to fall apart.

Cobb and countless designers, engineers, and construction workers had not properly accounted for the variations in weather that Boston experiences year-round. As the weather went from extreme heat in the summer to below freezing in the winter the air between the inner and outer glass panels would expand or contract, putting stress on the outer panes of glass, causing a total of 62 windows to fall hundreds of feet to shatter on the sidewalk. Besides endangering the lives of those walking near the building, this oversight cost millions of dollars to fix and led to a public-relations nightmare. With a little extra planning and knowledge of materials science and engineering, each of these issues could have been avoided.

Put yourself in the shoes of Henry Cobb, but instead of building a skyscraper you are building your career. In a sense, each of us is the architect, engineer, and builder of our own careers. We choose the tools to utilize and the design to build.

Unlike actual architects who go through years of training before designing a building and have the opportunity to create concepts for numerous structures throughout years in the profession, we come into our careers without much perspective and with only one shot at constructing our building. It is because of this reality that it is so important to find ways to give ourselves a leg up and increase our likelihood for success.

In the pages that follow we will go through 25 attributes that, when properly developed, will give you a unique advantage over your peers in being successful in the working world. Think of these attributes as tools and skills that will allow you to move up the corporate ladder more quickly, while giving you the ability to take more control of the path your career takes.

To help better understand the 25 attributes, let's look at them through the lens of two distinct characters.

The *STAR*

The Successful Young Professional is a *STAR*—**S**avvy, **T**enacious, **A**daptive, and **R**esourceful. She is a hip and independent woman who is determined to make the most out of her career. She lives in the city, recently completed her first marathon, and tutors kids in an after-school program. She dresses and acts professionally and always looks "put together."

She recognizes that she doesn't know it all and is willing to take the lead in making her career exactly what she wants it to be. She sets goals, utilizes mentors, and attacks opportunity. She realizes that taking calculated risks is important and is always conscious about what she does. She is also a lifelong learner, continuously looking for learning opportunities.

The *DOPE*

The opposite of the *STAR* is the *DOPE*. The *DOPE* is someone who **D**isses **O**pportunity, **P**otential, and **E**arnings. He is a smart guy who knows what it takes to be successful; for some reason, though, he chooses not to put in the extra effort to get there. He never goes an hour without checking Facebook and often wastes time. Maybe it's laziness. Maybe it's a lack of passion. Despite some moments of genius, he is generally inconsistent.

The **DOPE** doesn't learn from his mistakes and tends to make the same ones over and over. He is unfocused, apathetic, and, at times, unprofessional. The **DOPE** misses out on opportunities and is passed over when promotions and bonuses are available.

The 25 attributes of the **STAR** are discussed through the metaphor of building a house.

In the process of building a house there is an underlying foundation, an interior structure, and the exterior façade. Each is important, and the building isn't complete without all the parts. Thus, the 25 attributes are broken into these three distinct sections: Foundation, Frame, and Exterior. Part II, *Laying the Foundation: It's What's at the Core that Counts* addresses how the **STAR** is:

1. Un-entitled
2. Patient
3. Flexible
4. A fast learner
5. A team player
6. A person who follows through
7. A person with perspective
8. Proud of the work she does
9. Self-aware

Think of these characteristics as the basis on which your early career is built. If you do not lay the right foundation, then problems will surface later in your career before reaching the level of accomplishment of which you are truly capable.

Part III, *Putting Up the Frame: It's Not Only What You Do, But How You Do It*, offers attributes that are analogous to the frame of the house, focusing not on *what* you do at work but *how* you do it. Attributes detailed in Part III include a person who:

10. Is customer-focused

11. Acts "as if"

12. Makes decisions

13. Shows creativity

14. Is resourceful

15. Sells

16. Takes action

17. Multitasks

These attributes are important even when no one is watching, and they are rooted in your own self-discipline.

Finally, Part IV, *Finishing the Exterior*, discusses outward attributes that are generally apparent to bosses, peers, and coworkers. These are attributes on which young professionals are judged. Having a strong mix of these characteristics will increase the likelihood of career success. The attributes in Part IV include a person who:

18. Communicates effectively

19. Has a positive attitude

20. Networks

21. Demonstrates professionalism

22. Has integrity

23. Is coachable

24. Gives back

25. Gets results

These attributes center on reputation and the perception others have of you, also known as your personal brand. Keep in mind that you may be able to fool others in the short term, but gaining lasting success and solidifying your reputation only come when you base your career on a strong foundation.

Whether you are building with brick, stone, or Legos, there are certain principles of building that are universal: plan properly, use the right tools, build with quality materials, and monitor your progress. When entering the work world your slate is clean; your plot is empty. You have a few raw materials and some of the tools you need to start building, but often do not have a blueprint for success. The characteristics in the chapters to follow will become the tools you use, the jobs you take on will be your raw materials, and the structure you begin to build will ultimately become your career. After revealing the details of each of these attributes, you will build your own career blueprint and put it into action.

In going through the 25 traits, remember to judge yourself on a spectrum. For example, it should not be a "yes, I can multitask" or "no, I can't multitask" diagnosis. Instead, realize that your skill level for each exists at a varying degree. The **STAR** would not score 100 percent on all 25 attributes; the *STAR* builds exceptional strengths in a few key areas and avoids being a *DOPE* in the rest.

As you read, keep in mind that you are the architect of your own career. You are the key driver of your success. No matter your age, your experience level, or how far you are into your career, the 25 attributes covered throughout the book will get you where you want to go.

Grab your hard hat and tool belt; let's start building.

Explore Online

Go to TheSparkSource.com, click on Resources on the menu bar. Once on the Resources page, find and take the first part of the STAR preassessment, for the Foundational attributes (Attributes 1-9).

PART II

Laying the Foundation:
It's What's at the Core That Counts

The attributes in the chapters that follow represent the foundation of the house that you are building. Each of these traits is core to the success of your career. It may be challenging to develop these attributes at first, but they can be learned. With time and conscious effort, you will internalize them. These traits are the concrete that holds the structure of the house in place. The foundation of a house must be strong and able to support the full weight of the house. If the foundation is weak then the house will begin to fall apart.

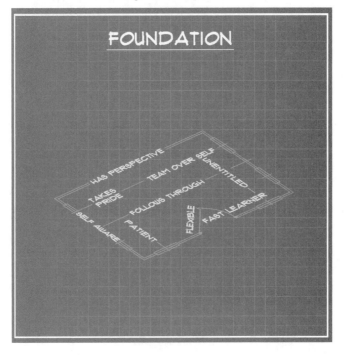

CHAPTER 3

Check Your Ego at the Door: Dulling the Sense of Entitlement

What to Expect: Despite an inherent belief many millennials have, we won't always be able to get what we want at work. We can't expect to continue to receive recognition just for meeting expectations. This chapter helps you get past the assumption that you will be praised for your accomplishments and that you automatically deserve to be in positions of authority and influence.

It is easy, when you are young, to believe that what you desire is no less than what you deserve, to assume that if you want something badly enough, it is your God-given right to have it.

—Jon Krakauer, *Into the Wild*

One of the consequences of such notions as entitlements is that people who have contributed nothing to society feel that society owes them something, apparently just for being nice enough to grace us with their presence.

—Thomas Sowell

It was the perfect job for me! Exactly what I was looking for.

I was hunting through my school's online job posting system and found a great internship position at a well-known company. I remember that the posting laid out some steep requirements. The position required a minimum of three completed internships (check), at least a 3.2 GPA (check), and a notable amount of leadership experience (I had been the president of multiple clubs and actually had taught a course for a few semesters on leadership that was sponsored by the business school, so, check). I figured I was a shoe-in.

Not wanting to get too big-headed, I spent a good amount of time crafting a memorable cover letter and adjusted my resume to fit perfectly with the job responsibilities.

More than a week went by and I finally received notice. I didn't even get an interview spot. *Are you kidding me!?!* I remember thinking. None of my friends even met the minimum requirements for the job and my whole compilation of college extracurricular experience screamed "leadership, leadership, leadership!" There was only one thing I could do: give the recruiter a piece of my mind.

I looked on the posting and found the recruiter's contact information. I proceeded to write the nastiest e-mail you could ever imagine. I really wish I had saved it somewhere to remember how upset I was. I am sure the prose was nothing short of epic. The e-mail said some things along the lines of: You are an absolute idiot. I am perfect for this job and you couldn't tell if a candidate was good if it was tattooed on his forehead! The company not only hires morons but is not interested in building a future and would prefer to let talented candidates go work for a competitor! I imagine I ended the note by referencing that I would find a way to get back at the company for their "mistake" later in my career.

Not my finest moment.

Just as I was about to hit "Send," a thought popped into my mind: *Maybe I shouldn't send this note.* First off, what was it going to accomplish, as I already didn't even get an interview for the job? Secondly, if this incident got around to my school's career center, it may hurt my chances with other jobs.

I decided to erase the entire e-mail and start over. I crafted a brief note explaining my interest in the position, stating that I would follow up with the recruiter by phone in the next few days to learn more about the position.

Two days later I called the recruiter and he said that he would be at my school's career fair the following day and that I should come to the company's booth to speak with him.

The next day, I scanned the large ballroom where the fair was being held, finally focusing in on the booth the company had near the center of the room. Resume in hand, I walked up to the recruiter, explained who I was, and said that he had asked me to come and speak with him. After a few minutes of talking he inquired, "What are you doing tomorrow at 9:30 a.m.?" "Nothing," I replied. He then told me to come in for an interview.

The next morning we went through the interview, and to make a long story short, I ended up getting the internship position. This internship then led to a full-time offer that I accepted. I have been working at the company—AT&T—going on seven years now.

Think what would have happened if I had hit "Send" instead of erasing and rewriting that e-mail. I would not be where I am today and would definitely not have been offered the internship or the full-time job at AT&T. I would not have served as regional vice president and would not have gained the tremendous experience I have thus far in my career.

Quick Tip

Save it to your drafts folder. If you are about to send an angry e-mail or one with some controversial opinions, save it in your drafts folder overnight. If you still feel good about the message the next day, then feel free to hit "Send."

At the time, I hadn't known that a majority of the candidates accepted to the program were MBA students, and therefore more qualified than I. All I focused on was what I thought I *deserved*.

Don't feel as though you are *owed* anything in your career. In the spirit of Larry David's HBO show, remember to *Curb Your Sense of Entitlement* (instead of enthusiasm). This sense of entitlement, a **DOPE** trait, is not a unique characteristic that only I had embodied. It is a trait with which a majority of millennials are plagued. We feel this way because of how we grew up. Our parents rewarded us for everything! In every single activity we were a part of, we earned a ribbon, certificate, or trophy just for participating. Every American youth soccer organization team I was on, Little League season I played, or Cub Scouts event I went to, I was given an award just for showing up. I even remember getting recognized for having good attendance at school.

I am sure many of you have a box collecting dust in your parents' garage that is full of certificates and other awards from Brownies, 4H, science fairs, sports teams, and so on. Positive parenting and being treated "special" created an expectation that we would be praised and would advance quickly in the workplace.

This is where myths #1 and #2 (in Chapter 1) come from. We expect to be on the fast track for promotions and huge raises solely by fulfilling our minimum job responsibilities. The way we were recognized and rewarded as we grew up has solidified this notion. We think that as long as we are good at our jobs, then we will get everything we want. These are unrealistic expectations and give us a false sense of entitlement. This feeling of entitlement, or *deserving* something *just because*, is not only bad for our attitude but can also be destructive for our careers. To avoid this potentially career-limiting pitfall, find a way to dull this sense of entitlement.

In order to quit feeling entitled to anything (and everything), first take a step back. Put the situation in perspective. Determine whether the feeling that you *deserve* something is created in your own mind or is based on something specific you were promised. For example, were you expecting a 10-percent annual raise because your boss specifically told you you would receive one for meeting a goal? Or was it because you heard that someone once received a 10-percent raise a few years ago? In reality, we do not have all the details as to why that person got the raise of that level of magnitude. He or she may have a different job title in a different department. Odds are we are getting the information through hearsay, as well. Unless we have some evidence, it is not a good idea to think we *deserve* the same raise.

The only thing we should expect is that we will need to work hard to *earn* recognition and rewards. Realize that there will be times when life isn't fair. You can work hard and *should* earn a reward or recognition, but that doesn't mean that you *will* get it.

Before ranting and raving about what your boss or company *owes* you, be the **STAR** and think before you hit the "Send" button. Stop yourself from being the **DOPE** by checking your ego at the door. If I hadn't learned this, my professional life and career track would be far worse than it is today.

Don't feel entitled to anything you didn't sweat and struggle for.
—Marian Wright Edelman

Explore Online

Because we are so used to being recognized for participating in things, in the Resources section of The SparkSource.com.

The *STAR* vs. the *DOPE*

The ***DOPE***... Expects a promotion every year because he deserves it.

The ***STAR***... Understands that promotions are rare and must be earned, so she patiently waits for the right opportunity.

CHAPTER 4

Your Career Is a Marathon, Not a Sprint: Developing Patience

What to Expect: There is no need to be in a hurry. If you build your career foundation too quickly, it will present issues later as you build more on it. Because we are used to instant gratification, patience is difficult for young professionals. This chapter illustrates the benefits of taking things one step at a time.

Smart is when you believe only half of what you heard. Brilliant is when you know which half to believe.

—Robert Orben

Keep high aspirations, moderate expectations, and small needs.

—H. Stein

43

Most millennials are accustomed to instant gratification. We are used to watching movies "on demand" the moment we want to see them. We communicate in real time via text, IM, Twitter, and Facebook. We like getting something instantly, right when we want it. Today's technologies enable this, but they also create a damaging sense of impatience.

Impatience can be advantageous when blended with an inner tenacity and desire to accomplish, leading you to attain even the most challenging goals. It can lead you to "think outside the box" and come up with solutions you hadn't even considered. But in a work setting, it can also create poor results, bad habits, and a tarnished reputation. The mix of impatience and sense of entitlement lead millennials to expect to move up the corporate ladder quickly, only to become frustrated when it doesn't happen soon enough. *STAR*s keep their impatience in check.

Besides my full-time job, I had always been interested in starting my own business. I saw it as a great way to make money and possibly even give me more control over my career, because I was the boss. This interest led me to start looking for opportunities to start side ventures. One of the first companies I started was a custom wedding invitation business. In concept, the business sounded compelling. As friends and coworkers started getting married, I had heard stories about how expensive wedding invitations were and how there was a market for a better model to design your own. Because weddings are a multi-billion-dollar industry, I saw potential. My business partners and I used the Dell customization model equivalent for wedding invitations: Instead of choosing your hard drive, memory, and processor, a bride-to-be would select the paper, ribbon, and vellum that fit her wedding colors and style. There were literally more than a billion different invitation style combinations. We also used the highest-quality paper and ribbon, painstakingly selected after months of searching.

From a business operations perspective we created a pretty solid competitive advantage. Assembling wedding invitations is not easy, and takes time. Having them made in the United States would have cost a fortune, leaving us no profit margin. Instead, we contracted with an overseas manufacturer to make the orders at a fraction of the cost. The orders were airmailed directly to our customers within a few days. We charged a domestic shipping rate and took the difference in the international rate out of our margin.

Just as the orders started to come in, the cost of oil skyrocketed and our shipping costs more than doubled, killing our margin. By the time shipping prices came back down the business was in triage and we shut it down.

I could blame the business's failure on the jump in oil pricing, but the real issue behind its failure was a lack of patience. We felt as though we needed to rush our product launch instead of working to get the business model right. I was also impatient about wanting to start a business. Weddings are great, but the core problem was that I was not passionate about the business. It was not something I could see myself fully committing to for years. Instead of waiting for the right business idea to develop out of something I was interested in, I was impatient and I went forward with a business idea I should not have. In the process, I overlooked some of the necessary steps to learn how to make the business successful, lost a lot of money, and expended a lot of valuable time. If I had waited for the right moment and built a better foundation for the business, I would have been more successful.

Although it may not always feel natural, being patient can pay off.

A few years ago, I was in the final rotation of AT&T's Development Program. I was managing a business sales team and things were going well. Unfortunately, as my rotation came to an end, I needed to find a permanent role and there was no guarantee that I would be able to stay in my current job.

Around that time, a regional VP from another department wanted me to come and manage one of his sales teams. He gave a pretty hard sell, telling me about all the benefits of joining his team. Yet from my investigation I found out the hours would have been longer (including having to work nights and weekends) and the pay wasn't as good.

I desperately wanted to be fully promoted to regional sales manager somewhere at AT&T, and this opportunity would have been a sure thing. Plus, I was a bit unsure whether I could handle the more complex product set that the business account executives in my current department were selling. I faced a hard decision.

Quick Tip

Choose the right company and job. Just because a company wants to hire you does not mean that it has the right culture or role that will allow you to grow. Be conscious of what you are looking for and be patient enough to search until you find it.

Instead of going with the sure promotion, I trusted that my current boss would find a team in our department for me to manage. I had to patiently wait for two months but it finally happened. I got promoted and was assigned to a better office in a better area, managing a better team. In this job I made more money than I ever had in my career, and my teams did exceptionally well, leading to recognition and exposure to company executives. None of this would have happened if I hadn't been patient.

After working in various sales roles for three years, I was bored with the job and wanted a new challenge. I really wanted to get a promotion, but promotions in my area were hard to come by. As the months passed my level of dissatisfaction and boredom grew higher and higher than I could have imagined. Finally I decided that I didn't need to find a promotion, realizing that even a lateral move would be a good change. A few weeks into my search I found an open marketing position. I interviewed and was offered the job. Just before accepting the position, a question stuck in my mind: *Am I choosing this job because I really want it or because I am so bored with my current job that I want to do something new?* I realized that I was getting impatient about the job-search process. I decided to pass on the job.

Four months later another job became available. It was a huge promotion and was in a department I was really interested in: business development and strategy. I had to work hard to prove myself to my potential boss, but he finally promoted me. The job was better than I could have imagined—the best position I had had in my career up to that point. I would not even have heard about the opportunity if I had been impatient and taken that other job a couple of months earlier.

Some months later, the business unit of the marketing position I passed up was sold to an investment firm. I literally would have been working at a different company today if I hadn't been patient.

As millennials, our "I want it now" lifestyle has led us to think in the short term. The business world perpetuates this with its focus on quarterly results. This "What have you done for me lately?" mentality keeps us from coming to one of the most important realizations of our young professional lives: that *we don't know it all.*

Because of my sense of impatience I believed that I deserved to be promoted every year. I had some great ideas on how to make AT&T even better than it was, and I felt that I had the right to be put into a high-level position of influence. As time went on, however, I began to realize how complex the business world really was and how even one bad mistake could scar your career. Moreover, as author Ken Blanchard points out, one in 10 people gets a promotion each year. Nine out of 10 times it won't be you.[1]

I would scoff at the idea that it would take more than 20 years to reach the VP level at AT&T. Only after a few years did I understand the importance of having a foundation of experience when making tough business decisions. I still think that taking 20 years to get to the VP level at a large company is a bit too long, but I realize the value in gathering more experience before earning that level of responsibility.

I am not suggesting that we all give up and accept that it will take years for us to reach the level of accomplishment we want. Instead I am pointing out that we should learn how to harness and channel our impatience. Sometimes impatience can be a good thing. The **STAR** waits for those moments of urgency to let her inner impatience go wild. She pushes herself and others to go faster and do better. She leverages her desire to get the job done now to come up with new and innovative ideas.

Use the best of what impatience has to offer, and set it aside when it's better to wait. Don't make career decisions based on the emotion and irrationality caused by impatience. Instead leverage logic and foresight. These skills will build inner resilience and help you successfully make business decisions.

A man can be as great as he wants to be. If you believe in yourself and have the courage, the determination, the dedication, the competitive drive and if you are willing to sacrifice the little things in life and pay the price for the things that are worthwhile, it can be done.

—Vince Lombardi

The STAR vs. the DOPE

The DOPE... Must have instant gratification. He looks for the easiest and fastest way to get the job done.

The STAR... Understands that timing must be right and that sometimes big accomplishments take a while to come to fruition. She patiently waits and considers the long-term result instead of the short-term gain.

CHAPTER 5

Staying Agile in a Constantly Changing Corporate World: Flexibility

What to Expect: Change is BAU (business as usual) in corporate America. In this chapter you will learn why flexibility is important and how to build a flexible working style so you can use change to your advantage.

Be firm on principle but flexible on method.
—Zig Zigler

Fact: The business world is in a constant state of change.

Global expansions, new competitors rising from every angle, technologies advancing and forcing out old business models—what some refer to as "change" should really be called "business as usual."

49

Luckily, compared to older generations, we are familiar with change, and often embrace technology and new ideas. This puts us a step ahead, although it is important that we do not let this agile edge diminish as we fall into routines and the "comforts" or our day-to-day jobs.

Organizational changes are to be expected. I remember one year my department had three separate organizational changes, which brought in three different VPs and unique culture shifts. It felt like the leadership of my team was a revolving door. There was a flood of new goals and objectives each time a change was made, and I even had to get brand-new business cards and change my voice-mail and e-mail signature to reflect the latest name our organization was given.

Returning to the house analogy, the stability and longevity of any building depends on the flexibility designed into the structure. Whereas steel and other building materials are very strong, engineers and architects know that there needs to be a certain level of malleability incorporated in a structure so that it can withstand the forces of nature, from wind and rain to earthquakes. If the structure is too rigid it will snap under pressure. Instead of fighting the elements, engineers have learned how to let buildings absorb some of these external forces (think about the core principles of judo or how to best catch a baseball bare-handed). Our careers should be constructed be like these buildings, able to sway in the wind instead of fighting it.

Think about your career through the lens of an improvisational (or "improv") actor. In a blog post I once wrote about how adopting an improv actor's mentality can be useful in your career. The first rule of improv is to agree with your fellow actors and find a way to progress the scene. In other words, the best technique is to say "yes, and," then contribute another line or detail to the scene. If you instead disagree with your fellow actor's idea for the scene because it doesn't match exactly how you wanted the scene to play out, then the scene abruptly stops or becomes confusing and disjointed. Similarly, in our careers, we must be flexible and adapt as our environment adapts instead of fighting change. We must embrace a new focus and redefined goals as change occurs.

The Jim Carrey movie *Yes Man* offers an interesting perspective on flexibility. Carrey's character was used to saying no to everything. Then, through a twist in the movie, he was forced to say yes to any question asked of him. This opened him to a world of new experiences and opportunities, changing his life. When you say no amid change, you are ignoring opportunities right in front of you. If you say "yes, and," like an improv actor, then you are not only being flexible amid change but you are also contributing your own ideas and passion.

Quick Tip

Don't be late. Be flexible with your schedule, but never be late to meetings that you commit to. There is no excuse for tardiness. If it happens more than once your excuses will fall on deaf ears, even if you have a valid one. People associate timely attendance with your level of engagement as well as how important you think they are.

Just as Jim Carrey's character in the movie began to realize, the **STAR** recognizes that she needs to think through changing situations. She realizes that she can't say yes all the time. She sees that there are certain things, such as integrity, on which she cannot be flexible.

I can say without a doubt that one of the keys to my career success has been my ability to be flexible. I utilize mentors, make self-development plans, and set goals. At the same time, though, I realize that I do not have full control of the world around me and I never will. Just because I plan something does not mean it is going to happen. In a previous job, I positioned myself for promotion and worked for a couple of years to put myself in the best place to move up within my organization, only to have all my efforts proven worthless as new management came in, sending me back to square one.

Some people view change as bad, but it can also be good. In order to take advantage of the good, you need to be flexible. For example, I did not plan on having the job I currently have, and I definitely did not map out the exact path to lead my career to where it is now. Instead, I saw an opportunity and was flexible enough to take advantage of it. Throughout my career, I often changed my plans and focus. For a while, I wanted to work my way up to being an executive vice president of worldwide sales, and then out of nowhere an opportunity to get promoted into a strategy and business development role surfaced. I took it. The *STAR* sees an opportunity and is flexible enough to take it.

A consultant friend of mine captured the idea well when he noted that each of our experiences builds on the last. Past and current experiences open the door for future opportunities. Without the expertise and foundation you are building now, you wouldn't be positioned for the future. You never know how an experience will help you in the future.

For example, in a project management role I had, my VP asked that I cold-call potential buyers in our area to sell them a new product we were about to launch: AT&T's Homezone (which we now no longer sell). Upon hearing this request I remember thinking, *This isn't in my job description.* Instead of making this an issue, though, I decided to go with the flow. The result was outstanding, and I beat all my targets.

A few months later I heard about a regional sales manager position that was opening up in another division of AT&T. I decided to apply, and then went through the entire interview process. I'm sure I was compared to other people who had actual sales experience. Luckily my future boss saw the small project I took on to sell that new product as proof that I understood sales. With my previous management experience he was confident I would be able to lead a sales team. He later told me that without this experience, he never would have hired me. Looking back, I did not know that I was going to be great as a sales manager, nor did I think that the cold-calling I had to do for that one project would open this brand-new door for me. If I had not been flexible and said yes to this change in my job description I would not have been promoted.

Taking a brief step back to investigate flexibility, we can identify how to master this trait.

What is being flexible and what is not?

Being flexible is taking a path that we didn't necessarily plan on taking. It is understanding that circumstances change and knowing that we must adapt. Being flexible is having the vision to see how we can use previous experiences to help accomplish new tasks, seeing that it can bring us closer to our goals.

For **STAR**s, being flexible is *not* changing core values and guiding principles. Being flexible is *not* discarding all the hard work we have done to do something crazy or stupid.

Why is being flexible important?

Simply put, being flexible will open your career up to opportunities that you never even thought of. It will allow you to consider new ideas and approaches to solving problems or reaching goals, because you will not be dead-set on always using the same proven methods.

I recall freshman year in college when a dorm-mate asked me if I was going to go to a business club meeting on campus that evening. I had other plans that evening, so I was reluctant. But I decided to be flexible and change my plans. I ended up going to the meeting and finding out there was an officer position open, for which I was selected. The following year I was president of the organization.

How do you develop flexibility?

The best way to develop flexibility is to realize that we cannot control every part of the present or the future. Once we stop insisting on having control our eyes open to new things.

The **STAR** develops the ability to recognize opportunity and quickly analyze situations. The **DOPE** is too narrow-minded and gets stuck on the career plan he once built that says he must be the lead project manager for a specific project that works in a specific department for his next job. Or he just lazily lets an opportunity go by because he knows he would have to work hard to get it.

Flexibility will allow you to look at the opportunity at hand and determine how it can help you achieve your goals in ways you had never thought of. You can develop flexibility by understanding that although the end goal may be fixed, the path that will get you there can take a course you never would have imagined.

Remember not to get too tied to how things are right now. Don't be married to how exactly you were successful in the past. When circumstances change (as they constantly will in corporate environments), *STAR*s change the methods and mentality they use to accomplish their goals.

Ride with the current as opposed to continually fighting against it. Flexibility can help you innovate and can make your job easier, in addition to helping you climb the corporate ladder quicker.

Let no one think that flexibility and a predisposition to compromise is a sign of weakness or a sell-out.
—Paul Kagame

The STAR vs. the DOPE

The DOPE… Fears new things and holds on to existing processes and ways of thinking because he thinks change is hard.

The STAR… Adapts quickly, taking key learnings from each experience. This allows her to stay one step ahead so she can adapt and take advantage of new opportunities.

CHAPTER 6

How to Be Successful in Any Position from Day One: Be a Fast Learner

What to Expect: In this chapter you will learn how to go into any situation, no matter how difficult, and succeed. Even without prior experience or education, you can master your job by being a fast learner.

Learn the rules so you can break them promptly.
—Dalai Lama

To learn anything fast and effectively, you have to see it, hear it and feel it.
—Tony Stockwell

Let me share with you a summary of my corporate work experience after college. I think you will quickly find a common theme.

Customer Care: Managed a team of orders-and-billing-service representatives (many of whom had worked at AT&T longer than I had been alive) who were supporting our top corporate customers that spent millions of dollars with us each year. High pressure? Yes.

* **Prior experience:** None. I had never worked in customer service and had never had employees who worked for me before. I also had never managed union employees (something that adds a great deal of complexity and paperwork).

* **Results:** I helped the team attain our highest marks for many of the key metrics, and I motivated the team to stay focused during multiple account reassignments and an office move.

Project Management: Supported a growing team within a regional consumer marketing group. I worked with outside agencies to develop marketing materials and traveled around to offer sales support to retail locations selling our products.

* **Prior experience:** Zero. I had never done any real marketing, nor did I know anything about retail operations.

* **Results:** The team reversed a decline in revenue for our major product line, and I was given a great deal more responsibility to run various initiatives.

Network Operations: Managed a group of technicians (all new hires) who were installing AT&T's newly launched Uverse television product, which the company was spending billions of dollars to deploy.

* **Prior experience:** Nope. I didn't know anything about the technology behind the service we were installing when I started. I was definitely not the type that had rolled up my sleeves to do any technical work before this, either.

* **Results:** My team was able to meet all targets for installations with a very low repair rate. We also benchmarked many processes to improve the organization's overall operations.

Sales: Led a team of business sales executives who sold the entire suite of AT&T's products to small and medium-sized businesses.

⋆ **Prior experience:** Nada. I had never led a team of sales-people before, nor had I really had much sales experience (and definitely not any business-to-business sales experience).

⋆ **Results:** My teams were #1 in our region for three straight years. I then served as regional vice president, leading an organization that includes numerous sales teams across an eight-state region.

Business Development and Strategy: Developed the future strategy for AT&T in emerging areas and built relationships with external partners to execute on the strategy created.

⋆ **Prior experience:** I think you can guess by now...absolutely none.

⋆ **Results:** I am currently in this position at the time of publication, and to date I have had a strong impact on the overall strategy for key growth areas within AT&T while bringing in numerous potential partners to develop products and generate revenue.

What is the common link? That's right: I had absolutely no clue or previous experience when I went into each of the jobs. Yet at the same time, I was able to figure things out and become incredibly successful.

I did this by remembering one simple principle: Be a fast learner.

The ability to excel when put into unfamiliar situations with no prior experience is one of the key ingredients the *STAR* uses to move up in a company.

I am sure you have come across similar situations in your own careers and have been forced to learn something quickly, just to keep up with your job.

The easiest way to become a fast learner is to think of yourself as a sponge. At the beginning of any project, soak up as much information as you can. As time goes on, you will get a better understanding of what is relevant information and what is not, but to start, be open to anything. Immerse yourself in what you are doing and find what you are passionate about in the job or project. Once you do this, learning fast becomes easy.

The **STAR**'s primary tool is asking questions. Ask lots of them. Your manager and peers think it is acceptable not to know the answers to everything when you are first put in a situation. They have lower expectations. The **STAR** pounces on this opportunity. The **STAR** knows asking questions will make her appear engaged and insightful. The process of asking these questions lubricates the wheels of fast learning.

While in my sales management role, I saw the value of asking questions firsthand with two young salespeople who started on the exact same day. One, who worked directly for me, had endless questions to ask: "How do you do this?" "What do you think about this sales strategy?" "Why are these processes this way?" and so on. Soon after, the questions diminished and his results took off, and he finished the year well over quota.

The second salesperson worked for a peer of mine and then for me after a reorganization. She was very personable and seemed to have solid sales skills. Yet she stayed quiet. She wanted to figure everything out herself. She later admitted that she didn't want to bother her boss or look bad for not knowing the right answers. Her results began to suffer and she soon found herself on a "performance improvement plan." Six months after being hired, when I began to coach her, I realized that she did not understand some of the key processes and procedures required to do her job. Though I did explain the right strategies to her, it was too late. She should have known how to do her job by that point. At the beginning there was room for excuses; six months into a job there was not. She eventually got laid off.

Don't be afraid to ask questions.

Quick Tip

Do your research: Before asking a question, always Google it. Use your tools to see if you can find an answer on your own before going to your boss or peers with questions.

Be alert. Keep your eyes open for lessons from all angles. This will answer questions you hadn't even thought of yet. Routinely, I find that external sources will help tell me the best way to do my job. Whether it is a peer in my organization, an article I read, or a fact that I glean from a report, there are lessons everywhere; you just need to be tuned in to hear them. Immerse yourself in the things you don't understand. Get advice from those more experienced than you (via mentorship, a common theme you will see throughout the book), and educate yourself on things related to your new job. Finally, don't stop at *understanding* a concept. Build on it by taking what you learn, and contributing your creativity and ideas to it. This will show that you take things a step further. You show that you truly understand your job and the culture of the group you are working with.

When I moved from being a technician manager, where I wore boots and jeans and talked almost exclusively in acronyms, to being a sales manager for whom the last week of the month was crunch time to close out sales in order to meet quota, I used the techniques I've outlined in this chapter to transition quickly into my position: I asked my boss and peers questions. I educated myself on how to be successful as a sales manager. I analyzed what made the top sales managers in my organization successful. I began to adapt to the culture of the team. Then, I tested out new management strategies, sharing the ones that worked with my peers.

The concept of being a fast learner doesn't only apply to when you first enter a new situation. It is an important skill to call on during periods of change. Regardless, be comfortable with asking questions and admitting that you don't know the answers. You will find that people will give you the answers and teach you things you didn't know.

Ultimately, to be a fast learner you need to believe that you can go into any situation and be successful (especially when you think you are going to be in over your head). As a fast learner, the **STAR** knows that no matter what situation she is in, she will find a way to work it out. Even more importantly, she understands that stretching herself by seeking challenging situations will help her grow and learn more, further solidifying the career foundation she is building.

The only dumb question is a question you don't ask.

—Paul MacCready

The STAR vs. the DOPE

The DOPE... Waits to be told what to do and gets frustrated when he doesn't get a concept right away.

The STAR... Proactively researches and finds out what she needs to know by asking questions.

CHAPTER 7

It's Not About You:
*STAR*s Make It About the Team

What to Expect: Instead of focusing on personal gain, you will learn how to focus on contributing your talents for the betterment of the group. Although somewhat counterintuitive, it is an amazingly successful mindset.

Individual commitment to a group effort—that is what makes a team work, a company work, a society work, a civilization work.

—Vince Lombardi

The abundance mindset: "I'm happy from the success of others, especially those closest to me." The scarcity mindset: "I'm threatened by the successes of others, especially those closest to me."

The more we share, the more we have.

—Leonard Nimoy

It was my chance. I found the perfect opportunity to make the other intern in my department look bad. My boss told me the deadline for my big project was moved up a day and to be sure to have everything ready to present to the company's owners. My boss also asked me to pass the message along to my fellow intern, let's call her Linda. I knew I had to reprioritize my time to meet the deadline. I also knew that I was going to conveniently *forget* to tell her about the deadline change.

Mean, yes. Unprofessional, I know. But this was war. Linda and I had very similar roles in the marketing department. She always did great work and seemed to be building a better relationship with the VP and others from our department. I had to find a way to make her look bad to give myself an advantage.

I have learned to control it, but I am a competitive person. I love to win, and often keep score. This led to some success but also colossal failures that have made me look like a real idiot. In this situation, competition drove me to do something I'm not very proud of.

Throughout the next couple of days, I became consumed with how to keep Linda from learning about the deadline change. I made sure to intercept all communication between other members of our department and Linda. I stayed at the office later than she did (so it looked as though I was working harder) and I made it seem as though I was ahead on my part of the project to get Linda nervous. Basically I exhibited how to be the **DOPE**.

Shortly before the meeting with the company owners, I determined that I was not going to have everything ready in time. I had focused so much on Linda that I neglected to put enough effort into my part of the project. And to my dismay, because of some personal commitments Linda had that week, she had finished her part of the project a few days ahead of time. She was unconcerned when she finally found out an hour before the meeting that the schedule had changed.

Naturally, she discovered that I was supposed to pass the message along to her. I had lost her trust, and that ended up hurting our ability to work together on future projects. I also looked unprepared in front of the company owners, with major gaps in my analysis.

Quick Tip

Open up a little. Sharing information about yourself to coworkers and clients can build a stronger relationship with them. They are able to learn what you are passionate about (hobbies and interests) and get to know you personally, which often makes them more committed to helping you in your job. But be careful not to share *too* much or get *too* personal.

After this experience I knew I needed to recalibrate and adapt my strategy. This led to one of the most impactful decisions I ever made, creating countless career successes. Instead of worrying about others, I decided to focus on two things: (1) doing my absolute best in all that I did, and (2) making it my mission to ensure the team (and its members) reached our shared goals.

I know to some this might sound naïve. Yes, there may be others out there who make it their mission to make me look bad. And there have been times when someone else took credit for something I did. Yet an exponentially larger amount of the time, others see this selfless strategy and find ways to recognize me for my efforts. My bosses see that I want to make them look good, which leads them to give me more exposure to company executives (not to mention stellar performance reviews and solid raises). My peers and employees see that I am focused on removing obstacles that keep them from excelling at their jobs and then support me in reaching my goals.

Quick Tip

Everyone is important. Treat your admins and anyone "below" your level with respect. You can learn a lot from them and they can help you overcome obstacles. They will be your best advocates or your worst enemies in your journey.

When you focus on the success of the team as opposed to yourself, you will see new ways to be a leader among the group. You can better identify gaps in your team's plans and can take on the proper roles to best contribute your talents to make your team successful.

Among other names, our generation has been referred to as the "me" generation. Many of us can be self-involved and focused on our own accomplishments and career path. Focusing on yourself is a short-term strategy that is not sustainable or rewarding. Once you let go of making yourself look good, then you will be the leader you are capable of being. Others will also take notice, and that leads to bigger and better career opportunities.

Here are a few simple ways the **STAR** successfully makes it about the team.

* **Recognize the contributions of others.** Being the eager beavers that many of us are, we are always looking for ways to show people how valuable we are to our company. Instead do the counterintuitive thing and praise others when they do well. This is a key part of making it about the team. **STAR**s know that when they give credit for good results to others, they empower others to support them later and help them accomplish their own goals.

* **Admit when you make a mistake and ask for advice from the team on how to get better.** You are human so you will make mistakes from time to time. Whereas the natural inclination is to cover up a mistake, it is best to acknowledge when you do something wrong. Then seek guidance on why the mistake happened and advice on how to ensure it doesn't happen again.

* **Align your goals with those of the team.** Even with this selfless strategy, personal goals are still important and should

not be neglected. But it's important to make your goals fit with those of the organization. If your boss sets a goal to cut project timelines by 25 percent, make it a personal goal to cut your personal project timeline by at least 25 percent. If your team's focus changes from one product to another, make it a goal to learn more about this new important product and take steps to master everything about it. Often your personal goal will only be a small piece of the team's goal, but it is essential to the whole. (*Note:* I am not suggesting that you adapt your personal goals to be primarily and solely about the team; I am merely stating that when you align some of your goals more closely with those of the team it will help you focus less on yourself and more on the task at hand and others' goals.)

This mentality has led me to do things like dress up as Santa Claus and roam a shopping mall during Christmas. On a few occasions it has hurt my social life as I had to work late into the evenings and some weekends to meet the requirements of a challenging role. It has even led me to take on some of the job responsibilities of peers to ensure they are able to complete a project to meet a pressing deadline.

But it was also this mentality that has led me to consistently attain the highest performance ratings on annual reviews and, more importantly, has led me to be promoted to reach a level within AT&T that most only reach in their 40s.

The wise man puts himself last and finds himself first.
—Lao Tsu

The STAR vs. the DOPE

The DOPE… Looks for ways to always be #1 at the expense of others.

The STAR… Knows the right role to play to make the whole team better than the sum of the talents of its individuals.

CHAPTER 8

I Hope We Fail:
The Importance of Resilience
and Follow-Through

What to Expect: *STAR*s understand the importance of follow-through. This chapter discusses why this is key to building a strong foundation for your career. You will also learn the one word to get rid of that otherwise will build a mental wall between you and the success you want to achieve.

One of the secrets in life is to make stepping stones out of stumbling blocks.

—Jack Penn

People hate abandoning the notion that they would coast to fame and riches if they found their talent. But that view is tragically constraining,

67

*because when they hit life's inevitable bumps in the road, they conclude
they just aren't gifted and give up.*

—Geoffrey Colvin

It was at the height of World War II in Europe when the British
prime minister took the stage at the Harrow School to speak on Oc-
tober 29, 1941. At one point in what became one of his most revered
speeches, he proclaimed, "Never, ever, ever, ever, ever, ever, ever, give
in. Never give in. Never give in. Never give in."

I don't want to over-dramatize or in any way compare our careers
to a global war, but Winston Churchill's statement rings true for
almost any **STAR**. The working world is full of obstacles, animos-
ity, and setbacks. Whether or not we have the mentality Churchill
speaks of can be the difference between career success and failure.

The word that best captures someone's ability to recover from
adversity and failure is *resilience*. If we give in before reaching our
goals too often, then we train ourselves to be okay with failure. This
leads us to focus only on accomplishing things that are easy. In the
face of adversity, we generally have a simple choice: either give up or
persevere and push forward.

What we, as millennials, have in the realm of creativity and
enthusiasm, we can lack in follow-through. The combination of a
sense of entitlement and impatience that we often have can lead us
to fold when obstacles arise. Plus, we are used to being told that it
is okay to give up. Many of our parents allowed us to flake on our
commitments if we didn't feel like doing them. The lingering message behind this mentality hurts how our generation performs in the
workplace.

Some of this repercussion is due to the challenges we face in
implementing ideas in complex and bureaucratic companies. As
young employees we often have little authority or resources to make
a difference. At the same time, though, much of this comes because
we give up.

DOPEs let ego get in the way when they succeed. Besides un-
inspiring others, an unchecked ego can lead to poor decisions and

improper risk-taking. Ego drives **DOPE**s to think they can do and say anything and still be successful. Many times life comes back and teaches them that this just isn't the case.

Eliminating negative messages you tell yourself is an important step in developing resilience and follow-through. *Can't* is the first word to eliminate from your vocabulary. **STAR**s know that *can't* is limiting and leads them to abandon their passions prematurely because they have yet to see any immediate results. Another word to eliminate is *try.* Eliminating this word from my vocabulary in the last five years has helped me immensely. *Try* is a word that we use to make ourselves feel good about failure. If we worked very hard to propose a project and get executive support for our ideas but ultimately it didn't work, we tell ourselves, "Oh well, I *tried.*"

In reality there is no such thing as "trying"; you either do something or you don't. Using the word *try* as a crutch leads to acceptance of failure, the **DOPE**'s recipe for underachievement. If you see an orange on the table and you pick it up, then you have picked it up. If you reach for the orange but don't pick it up, then you aren't *trying* to grab the orange; you actually didn't grab it. Jedi Master Yoda captures this message perfectly in *Star Wars: The Empire Strikes Back* when he says, "Do, or do not. There is no try."

No matter how hard you work you won't always be successful. You will fail.

Years ago there was a man who came up with an idea he that he wanted to sell to restaurants. Despite being well into his 60s, he embarked on a journey because he believed what he was selling was the right recipe for success. He was turned down 1,009 times.

Yet after all 1,009 attempts he picked himself back up, dusted himself off, and found someone new to ask. Finally, the 1,010th time he found a buyer. His name was Harland David Sanders, and he was the founder of Kentucky Fried Chicken and the creator of the restaurant chain's original fried chicken recipe. Colonial Sanders acted just like the **STAR** would: He never gave up. As the Colonel shows us, you are never too old to be a **STAR**.

Failure helps.

Whereas I do not wish any bad things upon us, I do hope that we fail.

I don't wish this so we can taste defeat. Instead I want us to learn how to overcome adversity, and prevail. When failures arise, I encourage us not to just give up and move on to the next opportunity.

If you are passionate about what you are doing, then keep getting back up no matter how many times you get knocked down. If you are able to take a lesson from each failure, then you will get closer and closer to success. In the face of repeated failure, inventor Thomas Edison said, "We now know a thousand ways not to make a light bulb." Adopt this mentality. If Edison didn't follow through then we might still be in the dark today.

Failing helps you learn. As Michael Jordan stated, "I have missed more than 9,000 shots in my career. I have lost almost 300 games. On 26 occasions I have been entrusted to take the game-winning shot, and I missed. I have failed over and over and over again in my life. And that is why I succeed." Michael Jordan has the **STAR** mindset. Failure is okay. It means you are taking risks, pushing your limits. What's important is how you react to failure. A true measure of the **STAR** is how she gets back up and pushes forward.

In building your career, it is important to use your experiences to figure out what you are passionate about and in what areas you excel. Yet often the journey to discovering your passions involves a great deal of adversity and failure. You can't expect that every job you take or every experience you have will be ideal or career-defining. The key is to persevere through challenges and find your next step.

Many students became used to getting good grades and being at the top of their class in high school. But once in college they took classes in which the curve gave 50 percent of the class a C or below. Half of everyone who was used to getting As got Cs, Ds, or Fs. This is where resiliency and tenacity really came out. Some gave up and accepted they would be middle-of-the-pack, while others pushed forward, putting in extra effort to ensure they would be in the top half of every class. This extra effort is the prime difference between the **STAR** and the **DOPE**.

As MJ says, your failures are why you will succeed.

Most of the important things in the world have been accomplished by people who have kept on trying when there seemed to be no hope at all.
—Dale Carnegie

The STAR vs. the DOPE

The DOPE... Takes obstacles as a sign that he is going down the wrong path, making an effort at first but then giving up once adversity arises.

The STAR... Fights endlessly until she reaches her goal.

Chapter 9

Finding the Lesson in Every Experience:
The Power of Having Perspective

What to Expect: In this chapter you will learn how any situation, good or bad, can be valuable in your career. You will get key insights into how to deal with both positive and negative outcomes and explore the best strategies to overcome obstacles.

Failure is an event, never a person.
—William Brown

When you lose, don't lose the lesson.
—Dalai Lama

73

I knew it was going to happen.

I had thought for a few years that it made no sense that we had two separate sales organizations selling to the same customers. Then, at the beginning of the year when both organizations started selling each other's product, the writing was on the wall: One day we were going to combine together. And with corporate reorganizations come risk, uncertainty, and change.

At the time, I thought that I would land on my feet. My teams had always been #1 and my boss's results were tops among his peers. Maybe I would get a few new people on my team, but that was it. It would be just like the other four "reorganizations" I had experienced in the previous couple of years.

I was wrong.

My boss was reassigned, moving halfway across the country. My entire chain of command came from the other organization we combined with. Every single person from my team was assigned to other managers, and instead of being assigned to the geographic area where my apartment and office were (which had been my territory for the last few years), my new area was almost 100 miles away.

It became clear that this wasn't a "merger" of two organizations; my organization got "acquired." My new boss showed favoritism to his previous team and left all the managers coming from my old organization with lower-performing people and tougher territories.

I had sincerely thought that my track record of success would have put me in a position to get what I *deserved*. What was worse was that three years of work I'd done positioning myself for promotion with my organization's leadership went down the drain.

I immediately learned an important lesson. I had only focused on getting promoted within my current department and hadn't worked to network with those outside of my team. I hadn't realized that I also needed to build relationships and foster future opportunities with other internal organizations and also outside of AT&T.

These situations happen every day and will likely happen a few times in your own career. Instead of complaining when something doesn't go her way, the *STAR* puts the situation in perspective. When things do not work out it is important to understand why.

I grew up regularly being reminded of the following statement: *To know and not to do is not to know.* In other words, if you learn a lesson but you do not adapt your future actions, then the lesson is worthless. It's as though you didn't learn anything at all.

Whereas the *DOPE* will make the same mistakes a few times over, the *STAR* understands the things that made her successful so she can replicate them. She sees the paths that led her to failure and works to avoid them.

Developing perspective goes beyond extracting lessons from a personal experience; it includes learning from what is going on in the world around you. Looking at issues, challenges, and market forces from multiple lenses helps you improve the foundation of your career acumen. Developing perspective includes the ability to take positive and negative situations and understand the key lessons from both.

Quick Tip

Read. There is no substitute for reading. From articles to books, information found here will give you key perspectives that will help you do your job better and build stronger relationships with coworkers and clients. Reading will help you learn things you don't learn from direct experience. Reading = Learning.

Here's an example of a lesson I learned: A friend of mine experienced some big problems with her coworkers. She had just transitioned to a job managing a team of customer service representatives and was struggling to get along with her peers. Her peers treated her like one of their employees instead of as an equal. She couldn't understand why.

As we talked it out, I realized that she was treating her employees like friends. She constantly joked around with them because she wanted them to like her (instead of motivating them to do their jobs). Because of this her peers did not to respect her and she eventually left her job, realizing that she wasn't ready to be a manager yet.

Instead of falling into this trap myself, I paid close attention to how I interacted with my employees when I was in a management role. I constantly reminded myself that I was there to manage, not find new friends. The lesson from my friend's failure kept me from having to learn the same lesson the hard way.

The **STAR** is able to take someone else's failure and accurately extract a lesson, improving her perspective without making the same mistake herself.

How you respond to tough situations really matters in your career. I have found during my short life that if I keep this "lens of perspective" in the back of my mind then I am able to get through some of the toughest situations. When you constantly look for a lesson in adversity, you are sharpening your sword and are always being a student.

One of the most satisfying feelings you will have in your career is when you successfully overcome a challenging situation. When I managed a team of technicians at the time of a new product launch (this time for AT&T's Uverse TV product), I was challenged mentally and physically. The hours were long: six days a week, often until after 11 p.m. In the first week of the job I logged in more than 1,000 phone calls on my cell phone to my 30 technicians. We had to figure out processes as we went along. "Business as usual" was pretty crazy. To top it all off, most of the technicians were close to my age and had barely any experience.

The job was not easy. In fact, I hated it. I worked six days a week and had no time to go out with friends (who parties on Sunday nights, my only night off?). All I did throughout the day was sit in front of a spreadsheet manually tracking all the jobs the team was doing, calling my technicians, and continuously updating a report to my boss's boss every hour. Occasionally, I would have to visit a customer who was really unhappy to convince him or her not to cancel our service. Things did improve (as the product got better and

I became more comfortable with my job), but it was a very difficult role.

Only later did I realize the great lessons I was learning from this job. In previous positions, I had always been the one promising the customer something. With this job, I had to *deliver* what someone else had already promised. It was a very humbling experience. Eventually, I moved on to another position, but I had become a stronger person and a better leader through this experience. From that point on, whenever I face a challenge in my job, I put the challenge in perspective and see it for what it really is instead of what I was building it up to be.

In nurturing this lens of perspective the **STAR** finds strength through adversity. **STAR**s realize that they can handle more than they thought they ever could, blowing the ceiling off what they once thought their limits were. Developing perspective is simple. When you are in any situation, don't focus on how good or bad things are going, but instead on the lessons you can learn. Be a sponge for those tips and tricks that will make you successful, and learn what mistakes to avoid.

The **STAR** also "fails forward fast." She is comfortable with failure, focusing on the valuable lessons that come from the experience instead of the fact that it was learned through failure. With a mentality that failure is acceptable, you are much more willing to take action. When you fail forward fast there is no bad result, only a sharpening of your skills. You learn what doesn't work, helping you get closer to mastering what does.

As you gather a portfolio of experience, your perspective will get sharper and you will become more resilient. Like the **STAR**, you will be quick to identify lessons in every situation, learning from other people's successes and failures instead of directly having to figure it out on your own.

Your career is a journey. From the beginning, the better you are at "failing forward fast" and learning lessons from your experiences, the more successful you will be.

Would you like me to give you a formula for...success? It's quite simple, really. Double your rate of failure.... You're thinking of failure as the enemy of success. But it isn't at all.... You can be discouraged by failure— or you can learn from it. So go ahead and make mistakes. Make all you can. Because, remember, that's where you'll find success. On the far side.

—Thomas John Watson, Sr.

Explore Online

Reading List: Check out the list of books recommended for all young professionals on the Resource page of the SparkSource website.

The STAR vs. the DOPE

The DOPE... Gets frustrated with failure and setbacks, and doesn't take lessons from failures.

The STAR... Sees every situation in a positive light, either as a success or a lesson to learn from that will lead to future success.

CHAPTER 10

It's "Not *Just*" What Your Title Reads:

Taking Pride in What You Do

What to Expect: Whether your job is fun or boring, stressful or simple, fulfilling or not, it is important to always do your best. This chapter explores why it is important to always put your best foot forward by taking pride in the work you do.

Don't be afraid to give your best to what seemingly are small jobs. Every time you conquer one it makes you that much stronger. If you do the little jobs well, the big ones will tend to take care of themselves.

—Dale Carnegie

My mother said to me, "If you become a soldier, you'll be a general; if you become a monk, you'll end up as the Pope." Instead, I became a painter and wound up as Picasso.

—Picasso

Every year the sales organizations at AT&T have a big kick-off conference. Thousands of people fly in from all over the world to talk about last year's results and rally around how the new year is going to be more successful than any past year. A few years back, we all convened in San Diego for the three-day event. As the event rolled on, we had executive readouts, big announcements, and a healthy dose of partying. Finally, we were nearing the climax of the conference: the special guest speaker.

Year in and year out, the event organizers would get a big-name person to speak to the group. And each year they would keep who it was a big secret. This year was no exception.

A few minutes before the speaker was scheduled to go on, I slipped out of the convention hall to use the restroom. As I looked down the corridor, I recognized a familiar tall figure. It was Chris Garner.

For those who are not familiar with the popular movie starring Will Smith, *The Pursuit of Happyness* tells Chris's story. It details how he literally went from being homeless to being a multi-millionaire. During the filming of the movie, my dad (who is an executive chauffeur for high-end clientele) drove Will Smith and Chris Garner to and from the set. Given this connection, I decided to walk down the hall and speak with Chris. He was incredibly nice and invited me to join him backstage as he was preparing to go on stage. As he was getting mic'd up he began asking me questions. He started by inquiring, "So, Aaron, what do you do for AT&T?"

Because there were top executives, VPs, and senior management at the conference I responded, "I'm just a sales manager."

Chris snapped back at me, "*Just* a sales manager? You're not *just* anything. The job you do is important to your company. You need to take pride in your job and be the best at it you can be. That's what true leaders do."

I stood there speechless. He was totally right. I shouldn't sell myself short. What I did for AT&T wasn't glamorous, but it was important.

That was clearly a ***DOPE*** moment.

The ***STAR*** takes ownership of the work she does. Even though she may not have a fancy title or the sweet corner office, it doesn't mean she isn't a leader.

Besides being patient and flexible in the process, you must take pride in what you do. When your job totally sucks, you need to take pride in your work. When your boss is a total jerk, you need to rise above and ensure you are doing your best. You must do this without expecting people to constantly tell you how great you are doing either. Even when you are excelling, this doesn't happen.

Quick Tip

Give a little extra. If you work hard and finish early, take advantage of the fact that you can get more accomplished with the extra time. Taking pride in your work is doing what is right, when no one is even watching.

A recent study showed that 46 percent of workers think that millennials are less engaged at work than other generations. What's worse is that 68 percent feel that we are less motivated to take on responsibility and produce quality work. This is a reputation that we need to lose.[1]

The amount of pride you take in your job day in and day out has an enormous effect on the quality of your work and the results you produce. I am sure you have been in situations in which you really don't care. This leads you to either get the task done as quickly and carelessly as possible, or procrastinate and put it off until the last minute.

STARs understand that the best way to find the next (better) opportunity in their careers is to be amazing at what they are doing right now. They may not see others watching, but they are. People will notice if you give 100 percent and take pride in your work.

In college, I took a student-instructed course on leadership. The class was incredibly insightful and gave me a great foundation for something I didn't know much about. Despite taking four other courses that semester, I made sure to do all the reading, and went above and beyond what was required for class assignments.

At the end of the semester, the course instructor approached me to attend a meeting. He was about to graduate and wanted to talk to a few select people about participating in the future of the class. By the end of the meeting, I was asked to be the course instructor. I couldn't believe it! As a freshman, I figured that I didn't qualify to teach a course. In response to my disbelief, the teacher explained that he saw how much pride I took in my work and how passionate I was about learning about leadership. This led him to present me with an opportunity that I never even dreamed of having.

I accepted the challenge, given my passion for leadership and desire to figure out how to make the class even more successful. I didn't need to have fancy credentials to teach others; I just needed to be passionate and to take pride in the material I was teaching.

Quick Tip

Take pride in yourself. Exercise and eat right. Eat breakfast every morning and take time for lunch. When your day gets busy this often goes by the wayside. It's important take care of yourself to be at peak performance.

I taught the course for the next four semesters and expanded it to become one of the most popular student-led courses on campus. It also was probably the single most influential experience I had in college that shaped me as a leader.

*STAR*s know that their careers are marathons and not sprints. Taking pride in what you do and maintaining a "not *just*" attitude is not a short-term thing. It doesn't just apply to your first job out of school; you must keep this mentality throughout your career, from job to job and from company to company.

Back at the conference, after Chris Garner went on stage and inspired the audience with the story of his life, he was signing copies of his book. I decided to buy one and get in line to have it signed.

When it was finally my turn Chris smiled as I walked up to the table. "Who is this copy for?" he asked. I responded that it was for me.

He turned the book a few pages in from the front and wrote in big letters "To: NOT JUST!" as he exclaimed, "That is what I'm going to call you from now on."

A few months later I received a call from my dad. He told me he had driven Chris Garner that day! My dad said that as he started to retell the story of the conference to Chris, Chris stopped my dad, questioning, "Wait, you're Not Just's dad, aren't you?" with a big smile on his face.

As a young professionals, we must remember to take pride in what we do each step of the way. You are not *just* anything.

Don't wait for an employer, friend, or mentor to show appreciation for your work. Take pride in your own efforts on a daily basis.
—Denis Waitley

The STAR vs. the DOPE

The DOPE... Sees a job or task for the responsibilities it has and the impact it makes on the greater organization, getting discouraged if it isn't significant. He gets discouraged when his job isn't what he expected it to be, and he lets his work performance suffer because of this.

The STAR... Sees any job or task as a building block that will be valuable in the future no matter how insignificant it seems. She consistently gives 100 percent because she knows that someone who has the next big opportunity for her is watching.

CHAPTER 11

Knowing That You Don't Know It All: Building Self-Awareness

What to Expect: This chapter discusses the cornerstone of your building: self-awareness. You will learn what self-awareness is, why it is important, and the four-step process of developing it.

People travel to wonder at the height of mountains, at the huge waves of the sea, at the long courses of rivers, at the vast compass of the ocean, at the circular motion of the stars; and they pass by themselves without wondering.

—St. Augustine

He who knows others is wise. He who knows himself is enlightened.

—Lao Tzu

Those who are at least somewhat familiar with the rules of many major sports understand that the ability to "pivot" unlocks possibilities to score. Whether it is your pivot foot in basketball, allowing you to rotate around and find a hole in your defender's guard, or the back foot of your batting stance in softball, allowing you to guide the ball to a certain part of the field, your pivot foot is your anchor. It is the tool you use to navigate your surroundings and better control the outcome of the play.

In your career this pivot foot is self-awareness. Self-awareness allows you to see the options you have in front of you while being flexible. It provides you with an understanding of where your skills lie and in what areas you need to develop and improve. In simplest terms, self-awareness is your ability to know and understand yourself, to see your own gaps, and to determine what characteristics you can leverage to be successful.

Besides the ability to execute and take action, knowing yourself is of the utmost importance in developing a successful career. In the "building a house" analogy, self-awareness is the cornerstone of your structure—of your career.

Psychologist Daniel Goleman singles out self-awareness as one of the important traits of effective leaders in his study of emotional intelligence. Self-awareness, or the ability to read one's own emotions and recognize their impact, is key to anyone's success. Self-awareness is the controller for self-regulation and inner motivation. Whereas Goleman's commentary focused primarily on emotions, the concept also crosses over to skill sets and personal characteristics. When addressing self-awareness, Goleman starts by identifying the need to recognize one's own emotions and their causes while realizing the connection between feelings and actions. Ultimately the concept of self-awareness centers on self-understanding, leading to self-control.

I was recently walking at Crissy Field by the Golden Gate Bridge near where I live in San Francisco. Despite the misty weather and growing wind, an older man had been sitting on the rocks for hours near the beach stacking different stones that had no business being stacked on top of each other. It was fascinating to see how rocks much larger and more oddly shaped than the ones below could be supported by resting at weird angles. I immediately was struck by the way what this (very patient) man was doing mirrored how I was feeling at that moment about building my career.

Besides the obvious fact that sometimes I feel as though I have no idea what I am doing and wonder if my struggle to find career fulfillment will be fruitless (or as useless as stacking rocks), the parallels are notable: In order to build the rock structure (a.k.a. your career) it is necessary to start with a large, flat foundation. I saw this older man had picked a large, flat rock as the base of his stack. To me, each rock he stacked represented a job that I had taken on in my career. Following the base, it is important to choose the next rocks (the different jobs you take on) carefully. If you choose a rock too quickly, even if it looks sturdy and has a cool shape, it may mean the entire structure will topple over like a stack of unbalanced Jenga blocks when a few more rocks are stacked on top of it.

The wind and outside elements closely match the political forces within the workplace against which you need to protect your stack of rocks (your budding career). From a distance, my career (that includes experiences in corporate strategy, sales management, marketing, customer service, and network operations) looked a lot like this structure: a bunch of experiences that do not really fit together, but that somehow built on each other. At times I reflect and think, *What experience comes next? How can I get it to fit with the rest of the diverse roles I have already played without everything falling over?* I am sure that I am not alone in this feeling.

Self-awareness is the steady hand selecting each rock and putting the structure together. Your ability to understand how your different career experiences build on each other and fit together is the same type of skill the rock stacker was using to determine what angles and what part of the rock below on which to stack the next. And the gentle but sturdy hands actually stacking the stones replicates your utilization of the skills you are developing with each experience you have.

Let's say you sit down next to this old man to build your own stack of rocks. Probably one of the first thoughts entering your mind is *Great, I am sitting here among a bunch of rocks. I have no idea how to turn them into an actual stack, let alone only know which rocks to choose.* In other words, how do you develop the steady hand the old man has? How do you develop self-awareness?

*DOPE*s wouldn't take time to reflect on the effect their actions have on their career. They would blindly go through their day-to-day routines, blaming external forces for misfortunes. They would develop the feeling that things are happening *to* them, instead of taking control. They would quickly stack a bunch of rocks on top of each other, eventually ending with a pile of rubble when they fall over.

No matter what level of self-awareness you have, there are four steps you can take to increase this all-important trait. When it comes to self-awareness, it's all about *you.*

* Step 1: Analyze Yourself

* Step 2: Test Yourself

* Step 3: Stretch Yourself

* Step 4: Remember Yourself

Step 1, *Analyze Yourself,* is about getting real about who you are. Write down five positive traits that describe you. Next, write down five characteristics that are "development opportunities" (business-speak for what you suck at or don't have any experience with). Next, take a step back and ask some people that you trust if you are getting the right read on yourself. Good sources for this step include mentors, close friends, peers at work, or people with whom you have done group projects with before. Keep the list of the top five positives and top five negatives that you just wrote down. As you read through this book look at these along with the 25 attributes and evaluate whether you are a novice, an apprentice, or a master craftsperson at each.

Quick Tip

Corporate Self-Development Resources: Many companies have tools available to employees that will help you learn more about your strengths, weaknesses, and personality type. Take advantage of these resources. They are often underutilized by young professionals. If you do not have access at work, there are basic versions of these resources online (many available for free). I recommend the Myers-Briggs Type Indicator (MBTI), 360° Feedback Survey, DISC assessment, and SkillScan tools.

Step 2, *Test Yourself*, focuses on improving your self-awareness. Take what you now understand about yourself and look for situations in which you can sharpen your awareness and validate whether you accurately classified these traits. You can compare it to improving your eyeglass prescription: For most developing self-awareness, the typical diagnosis is far-sightedness. Generally, you are not able to see how you are communicating. Learn to think in the here and now, and become aware of what you are doing while you are doing it. Resist falling into autopilot and stay in the moment, even when you are in the midst of routines. Often, self-awareness will come not just from how you act but also from how you react.

Step 3, *Stretch Yourself*, is centered on taking your skills further and mitigating or eliminating the gaps that you are aware of. I realized early on in my career that as a competitive person I discouraged my peers from teaming with me and cooperating to meet objectives. Stretching myself, I decided to integrate a few (at first uncomfortable) habits of proactively sharing best practices with my peers and admitting that I was struggling in certain areas, ultimately coming to them for advice.

Quick Tip

Keep a journal. While reading Richard Branson's autobiography, *Losing My Virginity*, a few years ago, I learned about this idea. Since then I have carried around (literally everywhere) a little journal where I write everything from my daily "to-do list" to business ideas and notes from meetings. This is a great way to keep track of your brain trust.

The final step, Step 4, is to *Remember Yourself.* Self-awareness is not a temporary tool to turn off and on. It is a continual secret weapon that will be the key to help you take your performance to a higher level in some situations, and help you avoid serious mistakes in others. Give yourself feedback and monitor how your skills are developing. This process also helps you avoid developing blind spots, areas in your skillset where you think you are good, but you are really not. Next, keep records of instances when you showed self-awareness and bring to light times when you didn't. Solidify these lessons in your mind and use them to build on your ability to leverage yourself when navigating through different life experiences.

Leveraging self-awareness allows you to become conscious of all the other things going on around you—the corporate politics and the opportunities for you to leave your mark and excel. Ultimately, self-awareness will help you see a path in the midst of a tough decision. The right answer will be clearer. You can understand your potential and the areas on which you need to improve. This sense of being self-aware will help you build your values and evaluate important steps in your career.

You are the only problem you will ever have and you are the only solution.

—Bob Proctor

Explore Online

Career Foundation Blueprint: On TheSparkSource. com, go to the Resources page to find a diagram and summary that details each of the foundational traits of the *STAR*. Then, find and take the second part of the *STAR* pre-assessment for the Structural attributes (Attributes 10-17).

The STAR vs. the DOPE

The DOPE... Doesn't take the time to understand himself and therefore has no idea how he succeeded or failed when he faced career challenges.

The STAR... Leverages strengths to consistently outperform her peers, correcting any career-derailing flaws. She always sets time aside to understand the good and bad traits she develops.

The First Nine Attributes of the STAR Young Professional

The STAR vs. the DOPE

1. *The DOPE...* Expects a promotion every year because he *deserves* it.
   The STAR... Understands that promotions are rare and must be earned, so she patiently waits for the right opportunity.

2. *The DOPE...* Must have instant gratification. He looks for the easiest and fastest way to get the job done.
   The STAR... Understands that timing must be right and that sometimes big accomplishments take a while to come to fruition. She patiently waits and considers the long-term result instead of the short-term gain.

3. *The DOPE...* Fears new things and holds on to existing processes and ways of thinking because he thinks change is hard.
   The STAR... Adapts quickly, taking key learnings from each experience. This allows her to stay one step ahead so she can adapt and take advantage of new opportunities.

4. *The DOPE...* Waits to be told what to do and gets frustrated when he doesn't get a concept right away.
   The STAR... Proactively researches and finds out what she needs to know by asking questions.

5. *The **DOPE**...* Looks for ways to always be #1 at the expense of others.
   *The **STAR**...* Knows the right role to play to make the whole team better than the sum of the talents of its individuals.

6. *The **DOPE**...* Takes obstacles as a sign that he is going down the wrong path, making an effort at first but then giving up once adversity arises.
   *The **STAR**...* Fights endlessly until she reaches her goal.

7. *The **DOPE**...* Gets frustrated with failure and setbacks, and doesn't take lessons from failures.
   *The **STAR**...* Sees every situation in a positive light, either as a success or a lesson to learn from that will lead to future success.

8. *The **DOPE**...* Sees a job or task for the responsibilities it has and the impact it makes on the greater organization, getting discouraged if it isn't significant. He gets discouraged when his job isn't what he expected it to be, and he lets his work performance suffer because of this.
   *The **STAR**...* Sees any job or task as a building block that will be valuable in the future no matter how insignificant it seems. She consistently gives 100 percent because she knows that someone who has the next big opportunity for her is watching.

9. *The **DOPE**...* Doesn't take the time to understand himself and therefore has no idea how he succeeded or failed when he faced career challenges.
   *The **STAR**...* Leverages strengths to consistently outperform her peers, correcting any career-derailing flaws. She always sets time aside to understand the good and bad traits she develops.

PART III

Putting Up the Frame:
It's Not Only What You Do,
But How You Do It

This section represents the frame in the house analogy. These nine attributes comprise characteristics that are structural to the creation of a solid career. These traits are focused around not *what* you do, but *how* you do it. Without these strong pillars supporting the structure of your house, it would have no shape or form and would crack and crumble.

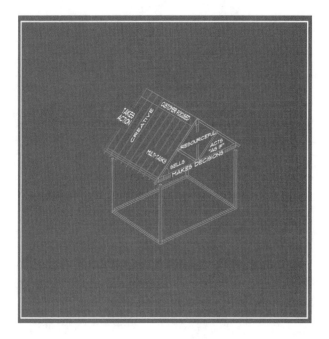

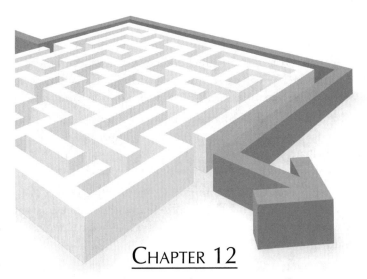

CHAPTER 12

The Goal of Every Job:
Serving Your Customer

What to Expect: In this chapter you will better understand what it means to be customer-focused. You will learn how to identify who your customer is as well as the benefits of always serving your customer first.

Quality in a service or product is not what you put into it. It is what the client or customer gets out of it.

—Peter Drucker

If you're not serving the customer, your job is to be serving someone who is.

—Jan Carlzon

Everyone can recall a terrible customer service story: Five calls in to a company's call center and still no resolution to the problem they created. Ordering something online, getting shipped the wrong item, and then having to pay a restocking fee to get what you actually ordered. These situations suck, in every sense of the word.

Now, think of the experiences in which you were truly satisfied, or even delighted. What characterized these experiences? Did someone anticipate your needs, give you more than you expected, and communicate with you in a professional and courteous way?

There is a reason why companies such as online retailer Zappos are incredibly successful: They realize that without their customers they would not make money and would basically have no reason to operate.

As a young professional, the level of customer service you give others is equally as important. I am not asserting that being the **STAR** is about making the customers your company serves happy. On the contrary, as employees we always have a customer of our own. Oftentimes this customer does not fit the traditional definition: Your customer can be an internal organization you support or a vendor that makes a component of a product your company sells. Your customer can literally be anyone.

A *customer* is someone who:

✯   Has influence on how you achieve results.

✯   Rates your performance.

✯   Provides you with something you need to accomplish your work.

✯   Pays you for the work that you do.

You can easily identify examples of external customers you serve; namely, the people or businesses that generate revenue for your company. But in non-external facing roles it may be harder to pin down who the customer is.

Quick Tip

Get to know your clients and coworkers. Remember the little details about their lives: If they like gardening, remember to ask about their garden come spring. If they have kids, ask if they have summer break plans with their family. Look up the most recent games' scores of coworkers' and clients' favorite sports teams. Doing so helps you connect with them. Even using something as simple as an Excel spreadsheet to track interesting things about people you know professionally can be effective in helping you build solid working relationships.

In my business development and strategy role at AT&T, I did not have responsibility for any external customer. Instead, my goal was to develop the future strategy for a division of the company and then help the business units responsible for implementing that strategy find potential partners. In this role, my *customers* were the business units for which I was initiating external partnerships. I would regularly meet with my customers to understand what their needs were so I could focus my effort on bringing them relevant companies. I also looked to take my role a step further, by researching market trends and bringing new ideas to the teams I supported. I made it my goal to keep them one step ahead of the competition. I created events with industry experts and emerging technology contacts to give my *customers* exposure to areas they didn't have time to investigate themselves.

No matter what your job is, one of your biggest customers is always your boss. Your boss decides your bonus and whether you get a raise. He or she gives you the coaching and resources to do your job, fills out your performance evaluations, and has incredible influence over you and your job.

You are one of your own biggest customers as well. That is why the **STAR** realizes that she needs to take care of herself and find ways to reward herself for accomplishing goals. If you are not happy it becomes exponentially harder to "delight" any other potential customer you must serve at work.

No matter who their *customer* is, **STAR**s use these steps to ensure outstanding customer service:

1. **Figure out what is important to your customer.** Success does not start by convincing customers to buy what you are selling; success starts with understanding what is important to your customer. Ask what their goals are so you can align your goals with theirs. Understand their job so you can ensure the support you give brings them closer to achieving that vision. In the case of an external customer, this may be helping them resolve their issues quickly.

2. **Set the proper expectations with your customer.** Setting accurate expectations is paramount. Don't over-commit. If your customer wants you to complete a task within two hours and you know it will take you four, don't promise to have it ready in two. Be realistic. Give yourself the time you need to do a great job. When your customer is your boss, let her know the support you need to complete a project. It is better to set a realistic expectation that your boss is less happy with than to tell her what she wants to hear and then not deliver. This is "talking the talk."

3. **Anticipate your customer's needs.** The *STAR* won't just give her customers what they are asking for. The *STAR* takes the lessons she has previously learned and applies them to the current situation. She anticipates what her customer needs, and provides it without being asked. Although this amounts to some additional time and effort that your customers might not always find useful, when you provide them with something that they do like it will go a long way.

4. **Deliver on what you promised.** Any customer appreciates when you communicate in a professional manner, but if you do not deliver on what you committed then your demeanor does not matter. Serving your customer is all about follow-through. If you tell a coworker that you will attend

a meeting for him or her, for example, then make sure to attend (and report back on what key points were discussed). This is "walking the walk."

5. **Help your customers achieve their goals.** For external customers your goal may be to get the product they bought to them on time or to immediately resolve a problem. No matter what their goal is, your job is to help them reach it. When you focus on the goals and success of those you serve, more often than not you will have positive results too.

6. **Monitor your customers' satisfaction.** Just as companies do, you should track how satisfied your customers are. The best way to do this is by asking them. A hot measurement companies use to monitor customer satisfaction is the Net Promoter Score (NPS).[1] It counts those willing to recommend a company to others and subtracts out all of those who aren't. Do the same with your customers. Ask them if they are willing to recommend you to others. If they aren't, figure out why not, and fix it.

One way to fulfill these six steps is to sketch out a customer service plan. Simply identify who yours customers are, determine what their goals are, and outline what steps you can take to support them in reaching their goals. Then, create a communication strategy so that you can share ways you are helping your customers reach their goals so they can be aware of your hard work.

Quick Tip

Titles can help. Knowing client job titles helps open up a world of answers. If you understand their department and roles, you can understand their goals and what makes them tick. This is great knowledge to have as you continue to interact with them.

In many cases, you will have numerous customers, and each customer will have his or her own (at times competing) goals. Do your best to balance your time and effort according to the customer with the most immediate or important needs. Finally, remember that with customers it is a two-way street: Although it is your job to help them, they ultimately will help you be successful.

As an employee your primary customer is your company. Your company provides 100 percent of your revenue (your paycheck), and finding ways to serve it can lead to increased revenue (raises and bonuses) as well as influence (job responsibilities and promotions). As a "company" of one, be the best at customer service, no matter who your customer is, and you will be the *STAR*.

The more you engage with customers the clearer things become and the easier it is to determine what you should be doing.
—John Russell, president of Harley-Davidson

Explore Online

On TheSparkSource.com, you will find a quick "customer canvass" template that will help you better understand and serve your customers while monitoring customer satisfaction.

The STAR vs. the DOPE

The DOPE... Thinks his main job is to accomplish goals determined solely by his title and job description.

The STAR... Knows that in addition to results, a satisfied customer is more powerful and more influential in getting to the next level.

CHAPTER 13

What to Do When You Have No Clue What You Are Doing: "Act as If"

What to Expect: As young professionals, we often don't have the answers or the breadth and depth of experience to know how to handle every work situation. The best response is to act "as if" you are an expert at what you do, no matter your background, behaving the way someone successful in this role should, in communication style, strategic thinking, and appearance.

Regardless of how you feel inside, always try to look like a winner. Even if you are behind, a sustained look of control and confidence can give you a mental edge that results in victory.
—Arthur Ashe

Act as if what you do makes a difference. It does.
—William James

It was a big day.

I was starting my very first day of work at my first job out of college. I recall all the preparation I had done the night before: I picked out my best suit and a nicely ironed dress shirt. I had a briefcase ready with all the appropriate office supplies packed in. I even made my lunch ahead of time. I had been practicing the introduction I was going to give to my new team for a week. I felt confident and ready.

Flash-forward 12 hours. My boss had just shown me my desk (although I didn't seem to get my ID badge situation straightened out for about a month). Soon after, I was standing at the front of a conference room with 16 sets of eyes intently fixed on me.

I had worked hard in college, both inside and outside of the classroom, but nothing could have prepared me for this. I was in charge of 16 unionized customer care reps who were doing a job I had no clue how to do—most of whom had been working at AT&T longer than I had been alive. To add even more pressure, we were supporting our top global customers who spent millions of dollars each year with my firm and I had no previous experience doing enterprise customer service. Being a fast learner is a key to overcoming this king of ambiguity, but there is another part of the equation that was equally important to mastering my job: acting "as if."

Acting "as if" means putting yourself in the same mindset as someone who is successful in your job. You want to *think* the way they think and *do* what they would do. Although panic and doubt can be byproducts of facing these ambiguous situations, acting "as if" you are qualified for a position will lead to improved results. The **STAR** develops a mentality that she can take on any challenge. This is also a fast track to getting more responsibility and moving up the corporate ladder.

If you are an outside salesperson at a software company, from day one you want to put yourself in the shoes of a successful salesperson.

You want to walk like they walk and talk like they talk. If a successful salesperson in your industry is aggressive and communicates in a direct faction, that is how you want to act. Some people call this a "fake it until you make it" mentality, but I resent the connotation of this statement. Acting "as if" you are good at your job is not about faking or misleading everyone; it is about taking the time to understand what makes someone successful in your position and then embodying everything that creates this success.

Quick Tip

Your appearance matters. Dress for the position you want, not the one you have. Watch out for over-using fragrance or accessories, but otherwise always look your best.

When I served as regional vice president of a sales organization at AT&T, I had never been in a position in which I had to manage people who also managed employees. This extra layer of employees creates a great deal of complexity and requires a different set of management skills. Success comes from leading *through* somebody and not just *at* him.

The ***STAR*** takes the following steps to act "as if" she is successful in her new position:

1. **Study Up.** The ***STAR*** learns what makes someone successful in the position she is in. These skills may include specific functional or system skills (from knowing the basic accounting principles to understanding how to access an ERP system such as Oracle or SAP), or certain characteristics such as communication and project management skills. She plugs into her professional and social network to find people already doing the job she is about to do. The ***STAR*** proactively asks other successful people in her job what makes them successful.

2. **Do a Self-Inventory.** Think, *What would a successful young professional do?* The **STAR** would first plug into her self-awareness to understand what relevant strengths and weaknesses she had going into a new position or project. From there, she would see the gaps that she needs to fill and identify people to help teach her what she is missing. Step 1 can help with this.

3. **Mirror and Match.** The concept of mirroring and matching generally applies to a method people use to influence others or increase likeability. The technique includes mimicking or copying someone's movements, body language, and tonality when speaking with him or her. In the context of acting "as if," mirroring and matching means understanding how someone successful in your position walks, talks, dresses, and acts so you can copy him or her. If you work in a company in the financial services sector and successful employees in your position dress in suits and ties; talk about financial indicators like ROI, EPS, and liquidity; and read the *Wall Street Journal* each day, that's precisely what you should be doing. In particular, learning how to talk just like someone in your position goes a long way in gaining the respect of others.

4. **Adapt.** When you don't know something or you make a mistake by doing or saying the wrong thing, it is important to know how to respond. When acting "as if," there will be times when you look as though you don't know what you are doing. The **STAR** overcomes this by having some go-to people and resources to quickly get answers to her questions. Rely on a mentor or coworker whom you trust to assist you with damage control. Remember, though, that it's okay to say you do not know all the answers.

In the movie *Catch Me if You Can*, starring Leonardo DiCaprio and Tom Hanks, DiCaprio plays the part of Frank Abagnale, a young con artist who successfully impersonated an airline pilot, doctor, and lawyer while amassing more than $2.5 million dollars from forged checks. To learn how to be a doctor Abagnale befriended a physician who was his neighbor. Once given the position of resident supervisor of the medical interns, he leveraged his resources by having the interns fulfill his job duties. Abagnale was also a great escape artist, showing his ability to adapt (Step 4), and was able to move on to other schemes without getting caught.

I am not condoning lying (or forging checks), but the movie (and Abagnale's true story) offers a perfect example of the power of acting "as if."

You will face many ambiguous situations early on in your career, and because you do not have a couple of decades of professional experience to call upon like your older coworkers do, you need to become comfortable with unclear situations. You must do this while gaining responsibility, trust, and exposure. Acting "as if" is the key tool that will not only get you in the right mindset to conquer the new challenge at hand, but will also convince others around you that you are comfortable with ambiguity and able to rise to the occasion.

Chameleons are a species of reptile that are able to blend in with their surroundings. If they are on a tree trunk their scales will change to look more like the color of the tree trunk. If they are on the rainforest floor, they will change to blend in there as well. As agile **STAR**s, we can blend into each new role we take on by adopting the actions, behaviors, and thoughts of those successful in this role.

Be a chameleon and act "as if" you are already the best at what you do. Act "as if" you accomplished the goals you want to accomplish and you will accomplish these goals much sooner than you think.

If you think you can, you can. If you think you can't, you're right.
—Mary Kay Ash

The STAR vs. the DOPE

The DOPE… Struggles to find out how to do his job effectively in new and ambiguous situations.

The STAR... Grasps what someone successful in this role would do and acts as she would, adding in a little bit of her own uniqueness.

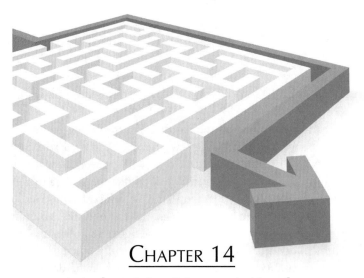

CHAPTER 14

Make Up Your Mind: Sharp Decision-Making Skills

What to Expect: It's natural to feel overwhelmed with the amount of opportunities available, with little insight on what the "right" path is. This chapter presents a framework for effective decision-making, while also discussing the benefits of decision-making avoidance.

All choices must be with a clear and attainable goal in mind.... Decisions made without clear goals in mind are likely to create confusion, resentment, and failure.
—Bill Russell

It is our choices...that show what we truly are, far more than our abilities.

—J.K. Rowling

Going through school, I was used to one thing: structure.

Even after finishing all the required courses in high school and college, though I got to take a few "elective" classes, I still had to choose from a list. Once I entered the working world I was struck by the infinite number of career paths I could take. I felt a lingering weight on my shoulders. How did I know which path would lead me to a fulfilling career and which was a giant waste of time? I constantly asked myself questions like "Would it be better to go work at a big firm or go work at a smaller company or start-up where I could get more responsibility?" These big decisions made it harder to make smaller decisions, like which car to buy or what clothes to wear to a big meeting. Why can't all decisions be like ordering from the In-N-Out menu? Single or double hamburger? Cheese or no cheese?

Among all the decisions we have to make, it is important to understand that there isn't just one path to lead to a successful career. There is no "right" answer, and it's natural to feel overwhelmed.

A couple of years ago, I faced a common career decision: Should I move to a new place for a job? I had to choose whether to move to San Diego or stay in the San Francisco Bay Area where I was living. I was forced to choose between comfort and the status quo and uprooting my life to move to a new area where I basically knew nobody. A million thoughts spun through my head, from determining whether I could move back to the San Francisco Bay Area later to weighing whether the exposure and added responsibility of the San Diego job would be better for my career. I was overcome with doubt.

There were many ways to approach this decision. Methods like listing pros and cons, creating a weighted analysis of all the relevant factors, and saying "eeny meeny miney mo" all crossed my mind. No matter the framework, it's best to take the following steps to successfully make difficult and career-changing decisions.

1. **Seek simplicity.** Your life gets more complicated as you get older. Besides jobs, spouses, kids, and mortgage payments add obstacles and additional factors to consider in making decisions. Find ways to eliminate the unnecessary and limiting parts of your life to create simplicity among the clutter.

2. **Prioritize.** I was recently at a career development meeting with an officer from AT&T. An audience member asked her how she was able to balance her work and personal life. When asked this question, executives generally waffle a bit and make the same point: that it's important to set time aside for family amidst the demands of a career. But this executive's answer was surprisingly refreshing. She noted that it's important to choose whether your career or family comes first. Once you determine this, it becomes much easier to make decisions. Write down your priorities. It makes the complicated task of managing tradeoffs surprisingly easy.

Quick Tip

When you want to move on to another job, make sure that you actually want the new job and aren't just looking to get away from the old one. Understand the root of why you feel a certain way about these kinds of decisions.

3. **Learn when to make a decision.** The *DOPE* will rush to make a quick decision. Take a step back and determine whether a decision must be made immediately. Postponing a decision until a more appropriate time can be a rewarding option. Consider the other areas of your life that will be affected by your decision. When looking to impress your manager to get the next promotion you could be prone to do whatever he asks of you in the process. This comes with sacrifices. In a previous position, I said yes any time my boss gave me a request. This extra workload led to competing

deadlines on a few occasions, and the quality of my work suffered.

4. **Break a decision into pieces.** Decisions are not always clear-cut yes-or-no scenarios. Sometimes you can get creative and find new options not initially available that create more value for you.

5. **Weigh the risk involved.** It is important to realize that even though decisions you make early in your career will affect where you end up later, making mistakes is not the end of the world. It is better to make mistakes that lead to key lessons earlier in your career when the stakes are not as high, rather than miss out on opportunities because you were too timid to make the bold choice. Identifying and taking appropriate risks can mean the difference between reaching the executive level and hitting a plateau early.

6. **Learn how to trust your gut.** Building and testing intuition is a key skill of the *STAR*. *STAR*s know their intuition won't always be right, but with experience it becomes more accurate.

7. **Act and adapt.** Making the decision is not the end. Act according to the choices you make and remember that things change. You can be flexible, changing your mind later. For example, within the first year after graduating from college, I took a GMAT study course, thinking that I wanted to get an MBA. I signed up for the course and began studying and taking practice tests. I was committed to going back to school. A few months later, I looked at my career goals and the steps I needed to take to get there. I realized in my gut that I didn't want to go back to school. So I stopped studying for the GMAT, and focused on my job and building my entrepreneurial ventures. Don't get caught up with what you *think* you should do or what others *feel* is right. Make decisions that carve out your own path.

These decision-making skills are not just for big life decisions; they also apply to your normal day-to-day work. Should you have a difficult conversation with a coworker who has affected the quality of your work by not doing his job, or should you ignore the situation? Should you skip a meeting to finish up an important project due at the end of the day? Should you provide your boss with genuine feedback about issues you see with her management style, or should you just say that everything is fine? These are examples of the many small decisions that come up every day.

Don't be crippled by small decisions. Make them quickly and thoughtfully. The *STAR* makes decisions based on justifiable rationale.

Getting back to my earlier example, I decided to move to San Diego after all, and it ended up being a great decision. Through the job there I learned effective project management skills and met some of my closest friends in the process. Afterward, I was even able to find another great new job and move back to San Francisco.

Decisions are a necessary part of life. Be the *STAR* by building your decision-making skills. You will get better at this as you build on your experience. And remember, no matter what choices you make, you can always adapt later.

Don't flinch. Never let them see you falter or consider or show your doubt. Make your decision and follow through.

The STAR vs. the DOPE

The DOPE... Waffles among many good options and gets overwhelmed when making decisions.

The STAR... Weighs all the options, makes a decision, and adapts when necessary, also recognizing when it is appropriate to put off making a decision.

CHAPTER 15

There Is No "Box" to Think Outside Of:
Creativity in the Workplace

What to Expect: Everyone has heard of the concept of "thinking outside of the box" but few know what it really means. This chapter discusses how to think creatively, why the box doesn't matter, and when it is best to share (and not share) these creative ideas.

The creative thinker is flexible and adaptable and prepared to rearrange his thinking.

—A.J. Cropley

When you do the common things in life in an uncommon way, you will command the attention of the world.

—George Washington Carver

This was outside the box. Way, WAY outside the box.

I buckled my belt, adjusted my beard, and stepped out of the bathroom into the hot lobby of the movie theater in the local mall. It was almost Christmas, and I was dressed up as Santa Claus to spread the word about a new product AT&T launched called Homezone.

I never expected that dressing up as Santa Claus would be part of my job responsibilities as a project manager. I shouldn't have been too surprised, though, as it was my idea. To launch the product, we set up a kiosk at the local mall. While I distracted kids by being Santa, our salespeople had a captive audience of parents to talk with. The strategy worked (but I won't wear a Santa outfit for 12 hours straight ever again).

Discussing creativity always sparks a reference to thinking "outside the box." The idea of "thinking outside the box" assumes that in order to be creative you must to think differently than you normally do. Although this provides a good visual analogy, it does not provide a helpful framework for how to think.

As millennials, we think differently than other generations do. Because we grew up in the age of the Internet, we are accustomed to finding ways to use technology to get what we want. Instead of assuming that we need to change our thinking, we need to leverage the creativity that we already have within.

Quick Tip

Document everything. You never know when you are going to need some piece of information. Save your sent e-mails in a folder for reference. Looking back on these records can spark creative ideas, while also covering your ass (CYA).

There is no "box." Instead, we all have a horizontal plane (or layer) on which we think and operate that is parallel to everyone else's. Some think on a higher plane and others on a lower one. Find ways to leverage your creativity to lift your thinking to a higher plane. This is important because your creativity makes you unique. The creativity of your ideas will also determine the trajectory of your success in the working world.

Creativity can be an effective tool in fulfilling your job responsibilities. Thinking creatively allows you to innovate and uncover new ways of doing things when you hit obstacles. This increases your likelihood of success. But creativity alone will not guarantee career success. Creativity should always be grounded and accompanied by strategic thinking. Strategic thinking connects the *how* to a creative idea. Strategic thinking focuses on implementing the creative idea through a mix of tactics and strategy.

In my business development role at AT&T I noticed an interesting market trend. I saw that if AT&T created and implemented a specific strategy, then five years in the future we would have a very high likelihood of success with an emerging technology. Unfortunately my idea was fairly radical. It was risky, but it also made sense strategically. I knew I had to do something about it. From speaking to a peer, I learned that if I used the typical process to share this idea (creating a PowerPoint deck and presenting it to my organization's leadership), I would not gain any support and other people would block my idea from ever being implemented.

I decided to think strategically, considering other channels could I use to gain support for my idea. I embarked on a grassroots campaign that included writing my first white paper, bringing in outside experts to offer another source to validate my idea, and building up a small community of internal supporters to ensure our strategies aligned. I even convinced a partnership to do a proof of concept of my idea. In time, my idea gained traction and support. Time will tell whether my idea was the right business choice, but I am certain that strategic thinking elevated the effectiveness of my creativity to a new level.

Expect some of your ideas to get shot down. Don't be discouraged though. Focus on learning how to communicate your ideas and gain buy-in.

Whereas creativity comes to you naturally, effective strategic thinking comes with experience and must be exercised like a muscle. After running a sales organization for a few years, I realized that my management acumen and tactical skills were well developed, but my business (and strategic) acumen suffered because I hadn't exercised it. After transitioning to a strategy position for my next job, I noticed that my business acumen began to come back and grew stronger.

Here are some ways to develop your strategic thinking and strengthen your creative muscles.

* **Seek experiences** that give you an opportunity to be creative while developing business, management, functional, and industry acumen. Ask to be put in challenging situations.

* **Test yourself.** Stretch your thinking by coming up with new ways to do things; challenge the status quo in your normal day-to-day. But remember that creativity alone may lead to trouble. Leverage your strategic thinking skills with this creativity and you are likelier to succeed.

* **Think through the risks and benefits** of your options. Determine the right scope of influence to gain acceptance of your idea, develop the plan, and then identify and leverage the right resources to make your idea a reality.

If you have a great idea that you are passionate about, then use your creativity to make it a reality. Forget those who don't believe. Remember, I used creativity and strategic thinking to turn an affinity for beer pong into a beer-pong-table business that I co-created, built, and eventually sold.

Operate on your own creative level. Screw the box.

Imagination is more important than knowledge.
—Albert Einstein

WU, WEIQI

Sat May 09 2015

The young professional's guide

33029097411623

Hold note:

The checkout period for Folsom and Sacramento Public Library 1-2 disc DVD sets is changing from 3 weeks to 7 days on April 6, 2015.

If I'm allowed as an employee to apply my creative juices in a new direction, you're going to get a whole lot out of me, including ways to save or generate more income. But if I'm only allowed to do the same thing in the same way day in and day out for years, then basically I've retired— I've just forgotten to leave.

—Joan Lloyd

The STAR vs. the DOPE

The DOPE... Sticks to common, tested methods to accomplish goals.

The STAR... Risks sounding stupid and challenges norms to uncover new and better business practices.

CHAPTER 16

Hard Work, the Smart Way: Be Resourceful

What to Expect: What is hard work and how can we make it smarter? This chapter discusses ways to leverage your resources to ensure you are successful.

There's no excuse for not being great.
—Tom Peters

When I was your age, I walked 10 miles to and from school each day, uphill, both ways. We didn't have the Internet, so I had to wait for weeks to get a letter back from my friends.

We have all heard a version of this story from a parent or grandparent at some point in our lives, referencing how easy our lives are compared to when they were younger. I don't want to pick a fight with older (and wiser) generations, but our lives are pretty tough, too. Information is coming at us a million miles a second. Technology, while great, consumes us and makes it hard to focus and get things done.

Despite generational differences, one thing hasn't changed: Hard work is still one of the primary drivers of success.

In the context of building a house, great blueprints and high-quality materials are meaningless without hard work put in to actually build the house. Hard work is the tool that makes the dream of a successful career a reality. The *STAR* not only works hard but also works smart, using the right tools efficiently.

Working smart is *not*:

* **Always working overtime.** Putting a lot of hours into a project does not always lead to the best finished product. Work smart and finish up early by thinking through the best process to effectively complete a task ahead of time.

* **Being all about work at the expense of your life.** Sacrifice is needed for career success, but it is important to give yourself a break (work hard, play hard).

* **Only putting in effort to be recognized.** There will be times when you put a lot of effort into a project that goes unnoticed.

* **Doing things for the sake of doing them.** Smart work is not crossing a bunch of "to dos" off your list. Doing work for the sake of feeling accomplished only leads to busy-work. Effective, smart work is purposeful. Doing things that do not get you closer to your goals is a waste.

Effective, smart work includes the following:

* **Efficiency.** Complete a task in the most direct way possible; don't waste any time. Clarify any questions ahead of time so you have a clear path forward.

* **Simplicity.** Don't create extra steps and complexity. Strip down to the core of what you need to do and focus on that. Think about Apple's iPhone and iPad devices: Instead

of many buttons, there is just one. There is also only a single price point. With the endless string of e-mails we receive and information we are bombarded with throughout the day, simplicity is key to helping us focus and not get distracted.

✱   **Resource utilization.** There is a reason that most large companies do not build all of their products from scratch: It is difficult and it takes a long time. Instead, companies partner with or buy other companies that help them serve their customers. This is the same as you seeking advice from someone with expertise instead of figuring it out on your own.

✱   **Purpose-driven work.** There should be a reason behind the work you do. Don't do something just for the sake of staying busy. Make sure that whatever you do gets you closer to your goals.

An executive at AT&T took the idea of working smart so far that he refuses to attend any meeting that (1) he has not received a well-thought-out agenda for, and (2) does not have a specified objective to be accomplished. Although appearing harsh, it cuts out any wasted meetings and makes the meetings he does attend more effective.

Effective, "smart work" does not depend on the hours spent, but on your level of engagement, resourcefulness, and ability to accomplish your goal.

Quick Tip

Leverage technology. Technology helps us work smarter. Leverage mobile apps, cloud services, and online tools to enhance your ability to stay in contact with others and do your job more efficiently. Apps like Evernote (and many others) have been incredibly valuable for me by tracking important information.

The goal of your work should be to make yourself more valuable to your company. Everything else is irrelevant.

When I was recruiting as part of my first full-time job, I was invited to a "pitch" event put on by KPMG. One of the activities was a group scavenger hunt in the financial district of San Francisco. My team was the first to jump ahead and start searching for clues. But although we got off to a fast start, we ended up falling behind and eventually lost. During the activity debrief, the organizers spoke to the winning team, inquiring about their winning strategy. They revealed that it involved taking a step back to determine the best process to take in searching for clues. They worked smart, dividing up responsibility by figuring out what team members had certain skills. This took a few extra minutes at the beginning of the activity, but they caught up with and eventually passed all the other groups. "Working smart" is not about speed; it is about efficiency.

When working smart consider both technology and people. As millennials, we have a tendency to depend on technology, always looking for ways to get things done faster. Despite the tools available, it is important to remember the human element. Asking others for advice is probably the best resource available. Leverage technology, but don't forget to take advantage of the experiences of others. This helps you pick up lessons much faster than learning a lesson on your own.

In your career you should expect to work hard, but do it the smart way. Otherwise you are just like older generations who are still always walking uphill, both ways.

Excellence is doing ordinary things extraordinarily well.
—John W. Gardner

Explore Online

The PRO section of TheSparkSource.com has great articles and other content aggregated from many expert resources to help provide you with all the career development advice you need.

The STAR vs. The DOPE

The DOPE... Wants the satisfaction of knowing he did it all himself, sacrificing and working long hours to get there.

The STAR... Sees the value in getting help from others and leverages resources to create efficiency and make work simpler.

CHAPTER 17

We Are All in Sales: The Importance of Asking for What You Want

What to Expect: You are in sales, no matter what your job title is. This chapter teaches you the benefits of effective selling and addresses the importance of asking for what you want. Whether it is in a salary negotiation, a performance review, or an interview, the people (with a solid reputation) who have the courage to ask for something are more likely to get what they want.

Everyone lives by selling something.
—Robert Louis Stevenson

Always be closing.... That doesn't mean you're always closing the deal, but it does mean that you need to be always closing on the next step in the process.

—Shane Gibson

Thanks to used-car salesmen and people pushing pyramid schemes, "sales" has gotten a bad name. People assume that anyone selling something is out to take their money in exchange for something they don't really need. Although some people do thrive in these situations, most do not like being given the hard sale and thus loathe having to sell to others.

But interestingly enough, we are all in sales, and have been for most of our lives.

Have you ever asked your mom if you could hang out with a friend, promising to clean you room if she said yes? That's sales. Have you ever interviewed for a job? You are selling the interviewer on the fact that you are the best candidate for the job.

*STAR*s know there is no way to escape sales situations, even when working in non-sales roles. Everything from asking for a raise to convincing people in your organization that your great idea should be implemented is sales.

Instead of avoiding sales, embrace it and use your sales skills to your advantage.

Quick Tip

Earn the work style you want. Convince your boss to let you develop your own work style, from letting you listen to music to giving you freedom to work remotely, by showing her that this environment will make you more productive.

At its core, sales is asking for what you want.

Remember, you are your own biggest advocate. If you are not actively looking out for your own best interests, then who is? Because sales is both unavoidable and important to your career, you need to figure out ways to develop our sales skills. First, realize that "sales" is not a bad thing. Then, take advantage of the control you have in your career, instead of letting your career "happen" to you.

A friend of mine had a year-long contract position at a large technology company. While most of her peer contract workers focused on doing their jobs to the best of their ability, she leveraged the *STAR* mindset by taking an active approach. She made it clear to her boss that she wanted to work at the company full-time, backing up her claim with hard work to show her value to the company. Only four short months into her contract she was offered a full-time position, while none of her peers were given an offer. Her clear goal to get a permanent position, her selling of her skills, and her persistent asking got her the job.

The key to harnessing your inner salesperson is to first figure out what you want. Among all the different career options you have available, this can be the hardest part. If you don't know what you want it is almost impossible to ask for it. After you have figured out what you want, find the right people to ask for help; if you are asking the wrong person, then you won't get the result you are looking for. Next, ask the question the right way. If you are asking your boss for a raise, provide the right evidence as to why you should get more money.

A few years ago I hired someone for a business sales position. I got him a 20-percent raise, and, knowing the salary of other team members, I was satisfied with what I got for him. A few days later he called me to discuss his offer letter. Despite his lack of previous business sales experience, he felt he deserved more money. He informed me that he had a baby on the way and had a large mortgage payment, and therefore needed additional money. He asked me for a raise the *DOPE* way.

First, he didn't thank me for the raise I had already gotten him. Second, he didn't provide any objective evidence as to why he deserved more money—a key to effective salary negotiations. If he had shared with me that he had an extra certification that was applicable to the job that no one else had, or if he was somehow more qualified than anyone else because of his previous experience, then I would have been more compelled to go back to human resources to get him more money.

Quick Tip

Smile. It's astonishing how powerful a simple gesture can be in getting what you want.

When asking for anything, be very clear about what's in it for *them*. People primarily care about themselves, so it is important to "expand the pie" to offer the person you are asking something valuable. In the case of this salesperson, if he had agreed to take a higher quota to help me get closer to my branch sales target, then I would have been more willing to fight for a larger raise.

It is important to ask the right way. As Percy Ross explains in his book, *Ask for the Moon and Get It*, you don't want to demand, beg, or offer empty compliments when asking for what you want. Instead, put yourself in the other party's shoes and find the best way to communicate and "sell" your idea the way they would want to hear it. As you get better at selling your ideas and asking for what you want, realize that you might actually get it. But be careful what you ask for, because it comes with added responsibility and pressure.

Challenge the status quo. Figure out what you want to be bold enough to ask for. When people know what you want, and you provide them with good reason to give it to you, you get what you want more often than you think.

Life is a cup to be filled, not drained.
—Anonymous

The STAR vs. the DOPE

The DOPE… Isn't willing to sell others on the value he has. He assumes that the answer would be no, and doesn't ask. He focuses on what he wants, instead of the other person's interests.

The STAR… Masters the ability to sell the value she brings to others. She asks the question and comes up with alternatives if the answer she receives is not the one she wants.

CHAPTER 18

Stepping out of Your Comfort Zone: Taking Action

What to Expect: Even in the face of fear, uncertainty, and change, the **STAR** takes action to move closer to attaining her goals. This chapter investigates the important role of taking action in the process of building your career.

Don't wait until everything is just right. It will never be perfect. There will always be challenges, obstacles, and less-than-perfect conditions. So what? Get started now. With each step you take, you will grow stronger and stronger, more and more skilled, more and more self-confident, and more and more successful.

—Mark Victor Hansen

You miss 100% of the shots you never take.
—Wayne Gretzky

I stood on the ledge, 15 stories above the water, halfway across the Auckland Harbor Bridge. I remember it being a breezy afternoon with barely a cloud in the sky. I slowly inched closer to the edge, and my knees starting to shake in terror as a reached the end of the plank. As I looked down I could barely make out any details in the water below. It was all a blur.

After standing frozen for what seemed like an eternity, I let go. As I started to tumble down dozens of feet in a fraction of a second, I began to wonder why I had decided to go bungee jumping in the first place. I had just literally jumped off a bridge, by my own will, with only a giant rubber band tied to my ankles to support me. It was an incredibly thrilling experience.

When thinking about bungee jumping, everyone focuses on the initial fall from the platform. The thing that no one ever tells you is that once you reach the bottom you are yanked three-quarters of the way back up in the air three or four times until you come to rest dangling upside down, your head just a few feet from the surface of the water.

Was the experience scary? Yes. Would I do it again? I actually did jump once more, that time backward. I don't consider myself to be much of a daredevil, but I do think it's important to experience unfamiliar and often uncomfortable situations. Although some would consider this to be masochistic, it plays an important role in my professional development. Experiencing uncomfortable situations challenges your limits. And you can only accomplish as much as the limits you put on yourself.

Quick Tip

Time-outs are okay. When a friend of mine is about to go into an important meeting, she always steps away from her desk for a few minutes to take a walk around the building and breathe. Stepping away from your desk reminds you to step into a different mindset—one in which you need to have a clear and sharp mind for the meeting ahead.

It's natural to get comfortable with your routines. After being in the same job for a while things can become pretty easy. You know what you need to do at work, you have proven yourself, and you are in the midst of the normal day in and day out. It's safe and predictable, so why would you want to change it?

You should change periodically because otherwise you are prohibiting yourself from growing. The best way to grow your skills and confidence in your career is to put yourself in situations that are outside of your comfort zone.

Jumping off bridges aside, when I started my first job out of college I was way out of my comfort zone. I didn't know anything about the job, and everyone who worked with me had been at the company for more than 30 years, compared to my three days. In response to this seemingly terrifying situation, something extraordinary happened. I learned my job and excelled. What's more important is that I took what in my mind was the limit of the situations I could succeed in and I completely blew the threshold off of it. It is one of the best feelings I have had in my career.

When you handle more than you ever thought you could, you build confidence and stretch yourself further to get even better. All of this starts with a willingness to push yourself outside of your comfort zone. The "comfort zone" is different for every individual, and it does not always have to involve life or career endangerment. Doing something as simple as joining a professional organization or getting involved in some after-work activity may be your version of stepping out of your comfort zone. Whatever your limit is, stretch yourself beyond it. Although there may be times when you don't succeed, you will develop a new attitude that expands your horizons and the capacity of challenges you think you can take on. Nike's world-famous motto encapsulates it best: Just Do It. Simple and straight to the point.

Inertia will develop in your career. It is better to have the positive inertia that creates momentum leading to multiple raises, promotions, and opportunities to build new skills and take on more responsibility. Negative inertia makes you idle.

Taking action more often and doing something you normally wouldn't allows *STAR*s to gain more experience. Without this action, there is no way to obtain the additional experience you get for doing something.

Each of your career experiences will help you somehow later in your career in ways you couldn't imagine. Think back to the old man stacking rocks by the beach. Although they may seem diverse, each experience from your career will be added to your "stack" of experiences that help you make more sound business (and personal) decisions as you get older. The more action you take, the better you will be at identifying good opportunities in the future.

*STAR*s are proactive. They look for what they want and take advantage when presented with the right opportunity. The *STAR* routinely say yes when her boss wants her to take on a challenging project. She takes action, building a diverse set of experiences. She gets promoted much faster than her peers, because she understands the importance of taking action and leveraging her experiences to push past her limits.

I hear and I forget, I see and I remember, I do and I understand.
—Confucius (via a fortune cookie)

The STAR vs. the DOPE

The DOPE… Lets opportunity pass him by because of fear and the comfort of sticking with the status quo.

The STAR… Steps out of her comfort zone and takes intelligent action in the midst of change and uncertainty, constantly challenging her limits.

CHAPTER 19

Become a Juggler:
The Art of Multitasking

What to Expect: The world is moving too fast to only do one thing at once. At the same time, it is important not to get caught up in juggling too many things at once. In this chapter you will learn how to effectively multitask while efficiently maintaining a high quality of work.

Most of the time multitasking is an illusion. You think you are multitasking, but in reality you're actually wasting time switching from one task to another.

—Bosco Tjan

Many people feel they must multitask because everybody else is multitasking, but this is partly because they are all interrupting each other so much.

—Marilyn vos Savant

What does a "typical" work day look like? First you get up, and then you get ready for work and sit through traffic to get to the office. Afterward, maybe you grab a drink with some friends or attend some kind of social or professional event. Then you go to the gym and eat dinner. Throw in a little TV, seeing what's going on with friends on Facebook, or reading a book, and you have almost no waking time left in your day. This doesn't even include time with family and friends.

Then there's the actual work you do day in and day out: juggling multiple projects, helping your customers, beating deadlines—not to mention countless meetings and conference calls to attend. Then there are the 100-plus e-mails many of us receive every day. Sometimes all of this work fits in nine or 10 hours, but often it spills into the evening.

All of this adds up in one thing: busyness.

The corporate world is moving at lightning speed. Technology has made many aspects of our lives easier, but it has also complicated our lives and distracted us from what is important. Because it is nearly impossible to slow down the pace of the world around us, we need to find the best way to deal with the overflow of information and our limited time. We all have 24 hours in a day, and all of this time will invariably be filled up. The tool that best helps us make the most of our limited time is multitasking. Multitasking is essentially the art of executing many tasks simultaneously.

There is a debate regarding multitasking. Last year AT&T had a leadership conference centered on the concept of the "Corporate Athlete," offering a framework to live a healthier and more balanced work and personal life. The framework said to limit multitasking and focus only on one thing at a time. The program pointed out that this focus will bring about better work performance. Although I see some merit to the reasoning behind this, I believe that multitasking *is* an important part of being the *STAR*. There are a few elements to effective multitasking that you can harness to be more successful. Effective multitasking involves creating a *system*. Technology is a natural tool to leverage for this. Everything from keeping an accurate calendar to building in reminders for all of the items on your to-do list will help keep you on track.

Quick Tip

Keep a to-do list. Every day I make a *Master List* of things I want to accomplish. Having my daily "ML" handy keeps my time and focus on track to complete the things I need to.

Time management is a driver of how effective you are at multitasking. *STAR*s set time aside to complete the tasks they want to accomplish and focus solely on what they want to accomplish, one at a time.

Make your system a tool that works for you. Every day there are ups and downs. There are tasks you have to complete that can't be done in one sitting. Often, you need input or information from other people that may be slow or have to follow process.

When I have many things going on that aren't getting done I look for a quick win. I take my daily Master List and choose something on it that I can get done quickly. It could be an e-mail I need to send or a call I need to make. Completing this simple task and crossing it off my list helps reenergize me and motivates me to continue working hard on my other open tasks.

Quick Tip

Take breaks. Set time aside on your work calendar without e-mail or conference calls to take a step back. This ensures that you are making effective use of your time and are doing things that are relevant and important to your job. This is also a great time to think amidst your crazy day.

Multitasking can also create variety in our professional lives. When I am doing a specific task and get really bored, having something else to do allows me to still be productive.

Using the "assembly line" technique is another part of an effective multitasking system. In modern manufacturing processes, products touch many hands while being made. There is no individual person who assembles every piece of a smartphone or single machine that builds a car. If this works well for business, why would it be different for us? If, for example, you are in a business sales position, it is a waste of time to take the company from the top of your customer lead list, look at its Website to learn about the company, search LinkedIn to see the background of the person you need to get in touch with, put together a proposal for the services you think you want to sell them, and then actually call the person. Instead, break any process down into stages that you can batch together. For example, take notes as you look through the Websites of 50 customers. Then search on LinkedIn for all 50 people you are about to call, and so on. You will build momentum and efficiency as you complete each step in the process.

The time of day that you perform each task becomes important, too. In this sales example, because you are calling businesses you want to make the most of the time businesses are open (usually 9 a.m. to 5 p.m.). The **DOPE** would spend all day researching companies' Websites and LinkedIn profiles and putting together proposals, only to have 30 minutes, from 4:30 to 5 p.m., to actually call customers—many of whom would already be getting ready to go home for the evening. Instead, do tasks outside of core business hours that don't need to be done while everyone else is in the office.

In addition to breaking down tasking like an assembly line, the **STAR** "templatizes" a task. Here's an example of this: I was organizing an event where I brought together executives from a few business units at AT&T to meet with both venture capitalists (VCs) and CEOs from 10 start-ups in the Silicon Valley. The event took about 500 e-mails to put together. Instead of sending custom e-mails to each and every start-up and VC firm, I created templates, highlighting the parts I would change/customize for each of them. Technology, such as "mail merge" in Outlook, also helps.

Being organized and using your time wisely will help you, but this alone will just lead to a bunch of work. As **STAR**s know, truly effective multitasking must be prioritized and tied to goals.

Once there was a philosophy professor who began to fill a jar at the front of the room at the beginning of a lecture without saying a word. He started by filling the jar with rocks a few inches in diameter. Once he couldn't fit any more in he asked the class if the jar was full. The class said it was. The professor then took out a bag of pebbles and proceeded to pour them into the jar. Soon the space between each of the larger rocks disappeared as the pebbles slipped through the gaps. He asked the class again if the jar was filled. After a sprinkling of laughter, the students agreed that it was now full.

The professor then pulled out a bag of sand. As he poured its contents in the jar the sand maneuvered through to the bottom of the jar, filling up the remaining space. "Now," said the professor, "I want you to recognize that this jar signifies your life. The rocks are the truly important things, such as family, health, and relationships. If all else was lost and only the rocks remained, your life would still be meaningful. The pebbles are the other things that matter in your life, such as work or school. The sand signifies the remaining 'small stuff' and material possessions."

If you put the sand in the jar first there wouldn't be much room for the rocks or pebbles. In other words, if you spend your time on things that are not important, then you will lose sight of and neglect what truly *is* important. This is particularly applicable in the context of your career. As you multitask, remember to complete the most important things. We shouldn't avoid or procrastinate on the items that affect our careers most, from networking to always learning new things, to instead focus on insignificant "to-dos." The time management of your multitasking should drive you toward freeing up time for what is most important.

Another important part of effective multitasking is limiting distractions. With social media and the dozens of apps on your smartphone, it is easy to become distracted from the task at hand. The **DOPE** takes his attention away from what he needs to accomplish. The **STAR** is aware of what can be distracting and shuts these things out.

Multitasking is an important tool successful people use to accomplish more and maintain variety in their careers. Don't let distraction keep you from fully paying attention to what you want to accomplish. Instead, break tasks into pieces and learn to balance multiple things at once.

Do the hard jobs first. The easy jobs will take care of themselves.
—Dale Carnegie

Explore Online

Career Frame Blueprint: On TheSparkSource.com, go to the Resources page to find a diagram and summary of the attributes that are structural to the house you are building. Then, find and take the third part of the STAR pre-assessment for the Exterior attributes (Attributes 18-25).

The STAR vs. the DOPE

The DOPE... Allows his mind to be in multiple places at once, always getting distracted from the task at hand.

The STAR... Focuses on one thing a time but does many things at once.

Attributes 10 Through 17 of the STAR Young Professional

The STAR vs. the DOPE

*10. The **DOPE**...* Thinks his main job is to accomplish goals determined solely by his title and job description.
*The **STAR**...* Knows that in addition to results, a satisfied customer is more powerful and more influential in getting to the next level.

*11. The **DOPE**...* Struggles to find out how to do his job effectively in new and ambiguous situations.
*The **STAR**...* Grasps what someone successful in this role would do and acts as she would, adding in a little bit of her own uniqueness.

*12. The **DOPE**...* Waffles among many good options and gets overwhelmed when making decisions.
*The **STAR**...* Weighs all the options, makes a decision, and adapts when necessary, also recognizing when it is appropriate to put off making a decision.

*13. The **DOPE**...* Sticks to common, tested methods to accomplish goals.
*The **STAR**...* Risks sounding stupid and challenges norms to uncover new and better business practices.

14. *The **DOPE**...* Wants the satisfaction of knowing he did it all himself, sacrificing and working long hours to get there.
*The **STAR**...* Sees the value in getting help from others and leverages resources to create efficiency and make work simpler.

15. *The **DOPE**...* Isn't willing to sell others on the value he has. He assumes that the answer would be no, and doesn't ask. He focuses on what he wants, instead of the other person's interests.
*The **STAR**...* Masters the ability to sell the value she brings to others. She asks the question and comes up with alternatives if the answer she receives is not the one she wants.

16. *The **DOPE**...* Lets opportunity pass him by because of fear and the comfort of sticking with the status quo.
*The **STAR**...* Steps out of her comfort zone and takes intelligent action in the midst of change and uncertainty, constantly challenging her limits.

17. *The **DOPE**...* Allows his mind to be in multiple places at once, always getting distracted from the task at hand.
*The **STAR**...* Focuses on one thing a time but does many things at once.

PART IV

Finishing the Exterior

We have all heard the phrase *Beauty is in the eye of the beholder*. The eight attributes discussed in the next eight chapters have less to do with *what* you do or *how* you do it, and more to do with *the way others perceive you to be*. In our house analogy, these traits represent the visible exterior of the house: A beautifully constructed house with a strong foundation and a solid frame but an ugly exterior would not be appealing.

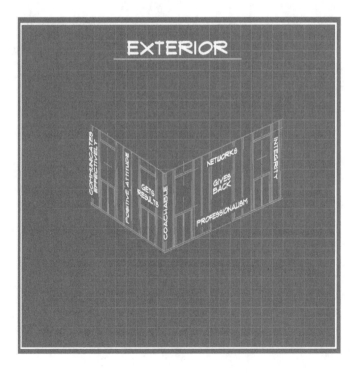

CHAPTER 20

Do the LEGWORK:
How to Be an
Effective Communicator

What to Expect: Even with e-mail, instant messaging, and video conferencing, you cannot hide your ability (or lake thereof) to communicate. Communication skills are the first and most important characteristic visible to those with whom you interact at work. This chapter teaches you how to communicate effectively while explaining the benefits of using reverse technology.

If you can't explain it simply, you don't understand it well enough.
—Albert Einstein

Information is giving out; communication is getting through.
—John C. Maxwell

147

The importance of communication cannot be overemphasized. Whereas each of the attributes discussed in this book has its own role in becoming the *STAR*, how effectively you communicate is the most important *visible* characteristic that will influence how effectively people think you do your job.

We all understand the importance of what we say or write in an e-mail. But just as with each of the attributes listed in Part III, communication is not just about *what* and *how* but, more importantly, the way other people interpret.

We have all seen how destructive bad communication can be.

Right after I graduated from college I traveled internationally for seven months, at one point staying on the island of Bali. I was backpacking with a buddy, and we had heard about a great spot on the beach in Jimbaran that served lobster and crab at sunset. We arrived a few hours early, and, upon seeing some fishing boats, decided it would be awesome to find someone to take us out to catch our dinner.

We found a teenager who spoke some broken English, and soon after were on a fishing boat headed out to sea. Not long into our trip the captain started asking us if we needed anything; he started with food, then drinks, then something to smoke. We shook our heads, saying we didn't. Then he started making hand motions about money.

That's when we realized we were in trouble. With most of our money and passports back at the hotel, we were pretty defenseless. While my buddy and I each silently freaked out, seriously thinking about jumping off the boat and swimming back to shore, we decided to confirm that we were headed out to catch lobster (making fishing-reel hand-motions).

The captain started laughing loudly. It turned out that the boat wasn't going out to fish but was headed for the island of Java, a 25-hour boat ride. "No, no, no!" we exclaimed. Somehow we ended up convincing them to send another boat out to get us, and we returned safely to the shore, amid heckling from the other fisherman. If we had communicated more effectively that we wanted to go fishing before getting on the boat, we would have saved ourselves from a stressful situation.

The *STAR* grasps that ineffective communicators are less successful and create more stressful situations for themselves than people who take ownership of their communication and confirm that others understand them.

Quick Tip

Always "close the loop." Even if you receive a straightforward request, follow up to show that you received the e-mail and will follow through on any actions outlined therein. Responsiveness doesn't just mean sending over your work; it also means showing that you're paying attention and updating clients/team members on your progress.

People get worked up over being misunderstood. As the **STAR** knows, a person with great ideas but an ineffective way of communicating them will be less successful than someone who has average ideas but shares them effectively.

An often-misquoted study by psychologist Albert Mehrabian found that 93 percent of people's attitude and feeling toward you and what you communicate to them is determined by nonverbal communication.[1] This does not mean, as Mehrabian adamantly asserts, that 93 percent of what you communicate is nonverbal, but that people's like or dislike of you comes not from the words you use but from your tonality and body language (55 percent from facial expressions and 38 percent from your tone). How you communicate affects how people feel about not only what you communicated but also about you as a person. Be conscious of your tone and physical presence when communicating with others.

Quick Tip

Be conscious when using acronyms. Every company and industry has its own unique language. Be conscious that not everyone you communicate with will understand all the abbreviations and acronyms you use. Spell it out for them.

*STAR*s master the following seven things in becoming effective communicators. *STAR*s do the LEGWORK to make it happen:

* ⭐ Listen
* ⭐ Evidence
* ⭐ Goals
* ⭐ "We"
* ⭐ Ownership
* ⭐ Reverse technology
* ⭐ Know your audience

Let's briefly look at each.

* ⭐ **Listen.** Most people think communicating only involves talking. The *STAR* knows that she needs to listen. People were given two ears and one mouth for a reason. Listening to how others communicate to you will let you know what is important to them and whether they are aligned with you or not.

* ⭐ **Evidence.** Communicating is not just about what you say or write. It is also about the supporting evidence you provide. Explaining the "why" behind ideas you share is one of the keys to getting buy-in.

* ⭐ **Goals.** *STAR*s communicate in the context of the receiving party's goals and what is important to them. People will listen more actively if you can master communicating the "what's in it for them" and tying your message to their goals.

* ⭐ **"We."** *We* is a powerful word. It connects you to your audience. Throughout the book I have used the word *we* instead

of *you* in sharing some of my ideas because we are all millennials and can relate to each other.

★ **Ownership.** The *STAR* takes ownership for what she says. She doesn't assume that others understand her; she checks to confirm understanding. When speaking to others, I follow up an important statement with a question like "Does that make sense?" to ensure people I am communicating with grasps what I am saying. When the audience doesn't understand, then I know I need to call on my creativity to find another way communicate my thoughts.

★ **Reverse technology.** Technology has done amazing things for improving our productivity and making our lives easier. At the same time, though, it can make communicating more difficult. When we can get caught up in communicating as efficiently as possible, the methods we use may confuse our message. E-mails and texts can be misinterpreted. There is no substitute for picking up the phone to make a call, or having a face-to-face meeting. I have seen in my career that once I meet with someone in person, he or she is more willing to support my ideas and help me accomplish my goals than when I just communicated with them via e-mail. This type of "reverse technology" helps build stronger working relationships.

Quick Tip

When communicating with executives, be brief, be insightful, and get to the point. If an executive wants to know more, he or she will ask. If you don't know the answer to the question asked, admit it and then commit to finding an answer. Then follow up.

★ **Know your audience.** It is important to understand your audience and make what you are communicating to them relevant. If I were speaking to a group of corporate executives

I would communicate very differently than if I was talking to a 5-year-old kid.

Let's see LEGWORK in action.

Here is how the **STAR** tells her boss that she is not going to meet a project deadline: First, she goes to meet her boss in person. (If they are not in the same geographic area then she would make a call, rather than sending an e-mail.) She then carefully chooses the right words to communicate, tailoring the message to her boss. She explains why she is going to miss the deadline, offering supporting points (evidence). She connects her statement with her boss's goals, and offers some alternatives to show that this bad news does not derail the team. She confirms understanding with her boss to ensure he is clear. Finally, she listens to his reaction and responds accordingly.

How effectively we communicate is the difference between being the **DOPE** and being the **STAR**. Doing the LEGWORK is the path to ensuring we are the **STAR** instead of the **DOPE**.

I remind myself every morning: Nothing I say this day will teach me anything. So if I'm going to learn, I must do it by listening.

—Larry King

The STAR vs. the DOPE

The DOPE... Expects others to understand what he communicates.

The STAR... Takes ownership of her communication. She ensures others understand what she communicates by adapting to her audience and following up.

CHAPTER 21

The One Thing You Will Always Have Control Of: Your Attitude

What to Expect: A positive attitude is a powerful thing that has an enormous effect on your performance. Even when you're becoming jaded by the frustrations of work, make sure to be cautious of the attitude you portray. This chapter discusses how to use a positive attitude to stay two steps ahead of your peers.

When we create something, we always create it first in a thought form. If we are basically positive in attitude, expecting and envisioning pleasure, satisfaction, and happiness, we will attract and create people, situations, and events which conform to our positive expectations.

—Shakti Gawain

153

The greatest discovery of my generation is that a human being can alter his life by altering his attitudes of mind.

—William James

You can't control the future.

No matter how hard you work, no matter how creative you are, no matter how well-thought-out your strategy is, you can only control your reaction to things.

Growing up, many of us have been told by our parents that we can do anything and that we are special. Although this kind of message has had a positive effect on us, it is important to understand that things won't always go our way. It's our reaction to challenging situations that determines how other people view us.

According to an ancient proverb, there once was a farmer who owned an old mare that he used to tend to his fields. One day, the mare escaped into the hills, leaving the farmer to tend to his fields alone. As the people in town lamented over the bad luck that had fallen upon the farmer, he responded, "Good luck? Bad luck? Who knows?" A week later the mare returned from the hills with a herd of wild horses in tow. The townspeople congratulated the farmer on the amazing blessing that had been bestowed upon him. In response, the farmer said, "Good luck? Bad luck? Who knows?" The farmer and his son began to tame the wild horse to use for tilling the fields. One day, the farmer's son was flung from one of the wild stallions, breaking his leg. Again, his neighbors and villagers chattered, speaking of the terrible turn of events. All the farmer said was, "Good luck? Bad luck? Who knows?" Some weeks later, a war broke out and the army went from village to village taking every able-bodied young man to fight. With a broken leg, the farmer's son could not fight and therefore was saved from battle.

Situations build on each other, and it is impossible to know what will come of a good or bad situation. This is why your attitude amid both good and bad circumstances will mark the brand with which others credit you. The farmer could easily have been upset when bad things happened, but he was wise enough to understand that good can come from bad and visa versa. You never know when a past experience will help you in the future.

Quick Tip

Always carry business cards. Different technologies can be effective, but business is still conducted through the exchange of physical business cards. The exchange of contact information increases the likelihood of follow-through and provides a good reminder of a connection. If you don't have business cards, use social networks or another electronic contact transfer. You may miss out on a big opportunity if you aren't prepared.

Don't be scared by your lack of control over your career. Embrace it and maintain an *I can handle anything thrown at me* attitude.

Just as in communication, the *how* is often more important than the *what*. The **STAR** knows that success lies not only in working hard and doing her job, but in having the right attitude while doing it. Your attitude will either inspire or discourage others.

A positive attitude has a double effect. The first effect is on you. When you have a positive attitude and a mindset that you can thrive no matter what, then when good things happen to you it reaffirms your positive attitude and outlook. In the same light, when bad things happen to you, instead of wallowing in sadness, focus on what good can be found in this crappy thing that happened. You will find a lesson that can help you build a stronger foundation to your career. It is important to understand that failures and adversity do so much more in making us stronger than when good stuff always happens to us.

Your attitude is also an active message to the rest of yourself, instructing you how to act. When people ask me how I am doing, instead of letting an automatic response kick in, such as "Good," people who know me would say I would respond that I am doing "awesome" or "amazing" or "spectacular." This serves as a message to myself. My brain is telling my body, "Crap, if I am doing 'awesome' then I better start to act and feel 'awesome,'" causing a physical response that affects how I communicate with others and gives me a more powerful presence.

A few years ago I faced a unique challenge when leading a sales team. Mid-year we were almost 30 percent behind the #1 team. Before I joined the organization, this other team had been the best team for a few years in a row. They were smart and savvy, and had a great sales territory. Yet somehow by the end of the year my team ended up becoming #1.

A case could be made that a few different factors led to this great turn of events, but I am convinced that the one thing that most contributed to our success was a positive attitude. A positive attitude is contagious, the second effect. My team wasn't the best or most experienced, but I drilled into the team that we could do it. I shared with them that I believed we were the best team and that by the end of the year I thought we could beat the other team. As time went on, everyone on the team began to believe we were the best and that we *should* be #1. This generated an individual and collective positive attitude. Then something amazing happened. All of a sudden this positive attitude led everyone to start acting in extraordinary ways. The people on my team began to help each other. They shared best practices and came up with new creative ways to sell more products. There were numerous times when I felt that all I needed to do was get out of the way and let this positive force take over.

Incredibly, after a reorganization split up the team the following year, my new team was even further behind the top team mid-year when I leveraged the same technique, and we were #1 again.

In the book *The Adversity Advantage*, authors Professor Paul Stoltz and Eric Weihenmayer assert that the success you experience in your career is directly correlated to how you handle adversity. Eric was able to accomplish something incredible—being the first and only blind man to climb to the top of the highest peaks on all seven continents, including Mt. Everest—because of his ability to conquer adversity with a positive attitude. There is no doubt that in your career you will encounter adversity. It may not be the same as climbing Mt. Everest, but obstacles will litter your path. You will experience challenges every day, and while getting past an obstacle is a goal, doing it with a positive attitude will reap true rewards.

A past coworker, who had a great education and a solid resume of previous experiences, was able to accomplish everything his job required him to do. He was smart and creative, and he went above and beyond what was expected of him. Yet when it came time for raises and promotion opportunities he was consistently passed over. One day he came to me asking why he had such terrible luck despite being able to fulfill his job responsibilities.

It was his attitude. The guy was a huge "Debbie Downer." He criticized any new policy that came down from the organization's leadership. He would complain about all the things he didn't like about his job and how much work sucked. He even went as far as openly arguing with his boss about how it was someone else's fault that he hadn't been promoted despite having great results.

The **DOPE** makes excuses and blames others. The **DOPE** holds a "pity party," looking for people to join in on pointing out how bad things are. The **DOPE** lets his negative attitude create a wall between where he is and the goal he wants to accomplish. Although some negative people may still accomplish great things, their path will be much more treacherous. Being negative doesn't motivate people.

The **STAR** does two important things to build a positive attitude. First, instead of focusing on a bad situation, the **STAR** looks for options and other solutions that can get her past the obstacle. A few years ago I was a listening to an executive at AT&T speak about change and handling difficult situations. He explained that instead of asking, *Why are all these changes happening?*, ask *What can I do to better adapt to the coming changes?* Instead of asking *Why it is that we never have the resources we need?*, ask, *What can I do to get more out of the resources I have, or how do I more effectively communicate why it makes business sense to get additional resources?*

He is right. There is always another solution or an alternate path to get to your goals. Don't dwell on the negative; create an opportunity for the positive by coming up with alternatives.

The **STAR** capitalizes on a few things inherent in all millennials when we enter the workforce: naïveté and optimism. She doesn't let herself become jaded by corporate bureaucracy and politics. Maintaining a certain level of optimism allows her to overcome challenges and become a stronger leader. She lets her naïveté work in her favor. Someone more experienced will undoubtedly say, "You don't know how things 'work' around here" when you introduce a creative idea or a new way of doing business. Leveraging naïveté, the **STAR** doesn't get tied down by the way "more experienced" people do things. Instead she focuses on finding the best way something should be done.

Remember, your positive attitude will help you overcome obstacles, will create new and unique ways of succeeding in your job, and will inspire other people to believe in you. Don't wait for "good luck" or "bad luck" to happen. Be the **STAR** and leverage your positive attitude as a tool to make you successful.

Weakness of attitude becomes weakness of character.
—Albert Einstein

The STAR vs. the DOPE

The DOPE… Gets caught up in the emotion or frustration of a bad situation, and lets his negativity show.

The STAR… Understands that her attitude affects her quality of work and the way other people view her. She keeps an open mind, looking for new options and positives in the face of adversity.

CHAPTER 22

The Road That Will Pave
Your Future:
Networking

What to Expect: No matter how great your work is, it is your relationships with other people that will control the trajectory of your career. In this chapter you will learn the do's and don'ts of effective networking.

The key to this business is personal relationships.
—Dicky Fox (from the movie *Jerry Maguire*)

It's not what you know, but who you know.

That's the famous saying that has been more than worn out whenever the topic of networking is brought up. Although the statement is true, in reality, it's not who you know but *who knows you!*

159

Networking is the key to connecting with others and letting them get to know you.

Evidence of the power of networking is abundant. It is one of the reasons why the rich get richer, but it's not always what you think it is. Many think of networking as going to a cocktail party or charity event, schmoozing with a bunch of high-powered people and exchanging business cards. Although this is a form of networking, it barely scratches the surface.

Quick Tip

Names are important. When being introduced to someone, listen attentively to hear his name, instead of focusing on how you are going to say your name back to him. Repeat his name in your head and use it a couple of times in the conversation.

The **STAR** knows that networking is not just about meeting people, but actually about *helping* them.

Here's an example: A former coworker of mine had been a top salesperson and was a huge proponent of networking. When he was first starting out, he joined numerous networking groups, from the chamber of commerce to professional organizations, finding his sweet spot in "leads groups." The sole purpose of a lead group is to provide a way for a group of professionals from different industries to give each other business leads. Each month his lead group gave an award to the group member who gave the most referrals. My peer made it his goal to win that award each month. Month after month he won this award, and soon the leads started pouring in. Because he had helped almost everyone in the group, they all began to make a concerted effort to build his business. Soon he was at the top of the stack among all salespeople, and he didn't even need to actively seek out sales with all the leads coming from the connections he made. All of this happened not merely because he joined networking groups, but because he made an effort to help others.

The **DOPE** assumes that due to a lack of experience there is no way he can help others. But no matter how much of a big shot someone is, there is always a way to help him or her. I once had the opportunity to meet a high-powered business executive from whom I wanted to get some career advice. Although I had no way of helping his business, I was able to make a few calls to some friends and secure an iPhone for him at a time when iPhones were all sold out. This meant a lot to him and helped me build a stronger connection with him. My efforts yielded me results in this case, but it's important to understand one thing:

When networking, you should never expect something in return.

There will be times when you help others out and get nothing in return. This can be discouraging, but the times when you do get help make these misses worth it.

There are two types of networking **STAR**s master: external and internal. Networking is not just meeting people in your industry through professional events, but is also about building relationships with people within your company. Often the latter are relationships that will give you the support you need to excel at your job. These people can also coach you on how to get a promotion internally. Without a network of supporters at your company, it's hard to move up to jobs with higher impact and responsibility. Also, networking within your company shouldn't solely focus on executives. Often, people just one level above you, at your level, or even below your level can help remove obstacles when you are in a jam.

Simultaneously, make sure to maintain healthy relationships with contacts outside your company. When it is time to move on to a new company these connections can help find your next job. In a previous job, I worked directly for a vice president who had worked her way up from any entry-level position throughout a 25-year career at AT&T. Then she was laid off during a sweeping reorganization. Left without many options, she told me her only regret was that she didn't spend enough time networking with people outside of the company.

When networking you should focus on helping other people, but it is still important to communicate what your goals and interests are. How are your contacts going to know that you may be interested in doing something they can help you with if you don't tell them? This piece of advice hits close to home for me. In the process of writing this book, I began to network with the most successful business-book authors. I started by asking them questions about some of the topics they had written on, letting slip that I was writing a book after we had been in touch for a while. When asking for advice on how to get someone to write an introduction for my book, Marshall Goldsmith (the *New York Times* best-selling author of more than 26 books, and recognized as the Most Influential Leadership Thinker in the world by the *Harvard Business Review*–sponsored Thinkers 50 Conference) volunteered to write the foreword that is included in this book.

Quick Tip

When being introduced to someone, say "It's nice to *see* you," instead of "It's nice to *meet* you." You never know, maybe you've met him before and forgot. If you say "meet" and *had* met him before, he will assume you don't think he is important.

*STAR*s understand that another key to networking is building relationships with people you aspire to be like. *STAR*s seek them out, find out how to help them, and look for ways to learn from them. When the *STAR* surrounds herself with people who have accomplished the things she wants to accomplish, she will become more motivated to reach her goals.

More than just getting what you want, networking is a great way to learn as well. Interfacing with people who know about areas you are eager to learn about broadens your horizons and gives you more insight than researching a topic on the Internet.

Here are a few more keys to networking success:

★ **Create relationships that are both professional and personal.** Get to know the people you are connecting with. Share stories about common interests. These stories will lead you to more things that you have in common, and having similar hobbies and interests improves your professional relationship.

★ **Make networking about the other person.** No one likes to hear other people brag, but almost everyone loves to talk about themselves. Ask the people you network with questions about their interests and accomplishments. Have you ever noticed that the conversations you walk away from liking the other person the most are those in which you did most of the talking? Letting other people talk about themselves in a networking setting will get them to like you more. Learning about them will also help you figure out ways you can help them (and ways they can help you). You need to be willing to ask for help. Sell them on helping you.

★ **Make others feel important.** Former President Bill Clinton and other charismatic leaders make those who talk with them feel as though they are the only person in the room. When talking to people give them your full focus and make them feel important.

★ **Follow up.** Networking is not just about meeting people and getting their contact information. Follow-up is very important. Find reasons to stay in touch. Pay attention to the things they are involved in, and check in to recognize their accomplishments and let them know what you have been up to.

★ **Connect people you are connected to.** Look across your network of connections and find ways to bring people together. This will not only make these people more willing to help you, but also allows you to help multiple friends at once.

★ **Don't judge a book by its cover.** Many people will treat executives or very accomplished people differently, putting them on a pedestal. No matter how successful someone is, he is still a person. Treat him like a person; get to know him as an individual and not just as a collection of accomplishments. A famous athlete would rather have a casual conversation with you than be asked for an autograph or a picture. Moreover, treat peers or people below you with the same level of respect when networking. You have no idea how they may be able to help your career in the future.

Remember that as you network it is about who knows you. Let others know you as the *STAR* who helps other people accomplish their goals and leverages other people to reach her own.

Help me help you. Help ME, help YOU.

—Jerry Maguire

The STAR vs. the DOPE

The DOPE... Expects others to help him succeed and rise to the top without helping them first.

The STAR... Sees that people will be inspired to help her if she finds a way to help them first, without expecting anything in return.

CHAPTER 23

The Most Visible Trait
for Any STAR:
Professionalism

What to Expect: Everyone has heard about the importance of acting like a "professional," but how can you balance being yourself and "acting the part" at work? This chapter goes over everything you should think about when it comes to being professional.

Professionalism is knowing how to do it, when to do it, and doing it.
—Frank Tyger

Professionalism: It's NOT the job you DO, it's HOW you DO the job.
—Unknown

A friend of mine is the head of the young professionals' employee network at a major financial services company. Regularly, he organizes after-work networking events for group members, often inviting company executives to attend and meet the company's future leaders.

At one event he made a sign-in board and posted it on the wall of the private room at the restaurant where the event was held. While most attendees simply signed their name and left a short message, as the evening progressed someone thought it would be funny to draw a giant phallus on the board. Others then contributed to the drawing by adding details.

My friend was completely baffled as to why these young professionals thought it was acceptable to act this way in the presence of company executives. The original "artist" in this story (as well as the contributing "artists," all **DOPE**s) had a misconception of what professionalism was. Professionalism is the conduct or qualities that characterize a professional, someone at the top of his game. Professionalism is acting appropriately in a variety of business-related situations. This includes the topics you talk about, the jokes you make, and the stories you tell, as well as how you communicate and present yourself.

Quick Tip

The boss test: Whether you are in the office or hanging with coworkers after work, don't talk about anything that you would not be comfortable sharing in front of your boss.

Why is professionalism necessary?

You need to separate your work and personal lives. You probably understand that you should not act inappropriately or too informally while at the office. But just because you leave the four walls of your office that does not mean you can drop all the generally acceptable behaviors of the workplace. This is especially true when you hang out with coworkers outside of work. Stories of what you do or say tend to make their way back to the workplace. Without professionalism, leaders at your company will not trust you in positions of responsibility.

How you act is a direct reflection on your company.

The first ingredient is self-discipline. Being professional means restraining yourself from acting as though you are back in college. Making a joke when you know it's not appropriate or treating someone disrespectfully is generally a **DOPE** move. Being professional is showing respect to other people and their ideas.

The scope of professionalism includes your dress, your demeanor, and ultimately how you act under pressure. For many, how you react to difficult situations is very different from how you act during normal day-to-day activities. The **STAR** ensures that she maintains the highest level of professionalism even in stressful situations.

It is also important to realize that different generations and cultures define professionalism in different ways. As young people, we may think sharing a YouTube video or talking about the details of our personal lives is fine, whereas others of older generations or different culture may not agree. Moreover, people from other cultures may see professionalism as strictly talking business and hiding any dissenting opinions. Understand that as a young person not only will older coworkers and those from other cultures have different ideas of what professionalism is, but they may also be predisposed to believe that you are a slacker because you are young and inexperienced.

Let me reiterate that acting professionally is not just limited to when you are in the office. Not long ago I was leaving my apartment complex to meet a friend for dinner. As I was heading out of the building, one of the security officers joined me in the elevator. I looked down and saw that she was watching a very sexually explicit video with some pretty nasty lyrics on her phone. As the elevator doors closed she immediately proclaimed, "Oh, don't worry. I'm on break right now." Whereas I can recognize her right to take a break, the fact that she was on break did not make her invisible to me, one of her customers. For some reason, even though she was still on the property, she felt the rules of professionalism didn't apply.

Quick Tip

When online, beware. Be mindful of what you say online related to your company and how you represent yourself outside of the workplace. It not only reflects on your company but can also come around to your boss and coworkers. Change your social networking site privacy settings to protect what you don't want to share. When in doubt, don't post it.

A key rule in developing and maintaining a sense of professionalism is to assume that someone is always watching. In the same way interaction can lead to a new opportunity for you, an act of unprofessionalism can derail your career. At the same time, though, remember that being professional does not mean that you have to be boring. Telling jokes, sharing stories, and having a good time is part of being in the workplace; it is just important to have a good pulse on the right and wrong times. Always be yourself.

I remember attending the orientation conference for a new job. All of the new hires flew to the company headquarters to learn more about our company and connect with our new peers. As part of the conference we had the opportunity to hear from the top 10 executive officers at the company. After hearing from the chairman and CEO as well as the chief financial officer, we had the chance to speak with our chief operating officer. After he had finished his prepared remarks, he opened up the floor for questions. One hand shot up at the back of the room. One of the members of my starting class stood up and stated, "Two questions. First one, totally unrelated to what you just spoke about, but has anyone ever told you that you sound exactly like Hulk Hogan?"

I have no idea what the second question was, but I remember that in response to her comment all the human resources staff either buried their head in their hands or stared off into space as though they had just seen a ghost. Sometimes being a professional means holding back when you are not sure if you should do or say something. This was definitely one of those times. Although I did think her question was hilarious, and it took every last shred of self-control not to bust out laughing, it was not the best example of professionalism.

A professional is someone who can do his best work when he doesn't feel like it.

—Alistair Cooke

The STAR vs. the DOPE

The DOPE... Believes there is no crossover between work life and social life.

The STAR... Understands that people are always watching and that even one slip-up can damage a painstakingly built reputation.

Your True Reflection: Integrity

What to Expect: Integrity is a guiding principle for great leaders and **_STAR_**s alike. But what exactly does being a person of integrity entail? This chapter offers perspective on this important topic.

That you may retain your self-respect, it is better to displease the people by doing what you know is right, than to temporarily please them by doing what you know is wrong.

—William J.H. Boetcker

Your life lies before you like a path of driven snow, be careful how you tread it 'cause every step will show.

—Lowri Williams

When I graduated from college I was selected to be the student commencement speaker for my university's graduation ceremony. A few months after graduation, as I was traveling internationally, I received an e-mail from a friend, explaining that he was auditioning to be the speaker for the undergraduate business school's commencement ceremony, and asking for advice and a transcript of the speech I had given. I gave him my speech, except for a poem I had recited at the end. At the time, I thought nothing of it, and continued on with my travels.

The following May came and I was back in my college town to visit friends and attend the undergraduate business school's graduation ceremony. As the students gathered backstage before the ceremony I went up to this same friend of mine, wishing him luck. I had heard he would be giving the student commencement speech. He seemed nervous as I went up to speak to him and even more nervous after I walked away.

The procession began and soon we were in our seats. My friend walked up to the podium and began to speak, his words sounding all too familiar. I noticed a pattern: 15 seconds of his words, 30 seconds of the speech I had given six months earlier, verbatim. Twenty seconds of his own words, 1 minute 15 seconds of mine.

I couldn't believe it. I was floored.

I had never felt so violated in my life.

There he was, someone who had been one of the VPs in a business club I was the president of two years prior, someone who was a teaching assistant for the leadership class I taught, standing in front of the entire class of graduating students completely and unabashedly plagiarizing my speech.

When I approached him after the ceremony, my state of disbelief only allowed me to muster up a smile and a brief "nice speech" retort.

In the week that followed, I sent the business school office staff a recording of my speech, asking them to compare it to their recording of my "friend's" speech. They confirmed that he had completely copied my speech (and according to the staff manager my execution of the speech was better).

While the positive attitude in me did its best to take the situation as a compliment, because the speech I wrote had been selected twice, ultimately it was a complete insult. This so-called "friend" of mine, who was a very smart and accomplished person, lost all of my trust, respect, and support through this one act, and it is something that he will never regain. He showed me that he had no integrity. It was that day that I realized that not everyone has your best interests in mind, even if they pretend to be your friend. Some people are selfish and tend to draw a pretty fuzzy line when it comes to what is right and what is wrong. This is especially true in stressful situations. This selfishness and blind desire to get ahead can cause *DOPE*s to toss ethics to the wind for a short-term gain.

I know that integrity is one of the least sexy topics to discuss, but is so important for young professionals. I struggled for a while to determine where to place integrity within the constructs of the "building a house" analogy. It really holds your entire house together. Integrity is foundational, core to the quality and longevity of both a house and a career. Lacking integrity is like having a beautiful house with huge cracks in the foundation. Integrity is structural as well. It is a key component of how you take on responsibility in your career. Integrity should be a companion to every decision you make. Dishonesty is like dry rot in the wood beams of a house's frame, creating weaknesses in the home's structure. Integrity is also part of the exterior of the house. While integrity is core to the *STAR*, having or lacking integrity is not self-determined, and is often decided on by those who interact with you. An absence of integrity is like having a house that has ugly paint and big, gaping holes in the exterior walls.

Quick Tip

Be careful what you use company assets for. Don't use your company laptop, printer, or phone inappropriately. Odds are your company is tracking you.

Integrity is fragile.

At one time a very accomplished regional VP of an AT&T sales organization, who had worked for more than 30 years with the company, was nearing retirement. He had a favorite regional sales manager on his staff who he was grooming to be his successor. It was understood that as long as this sales manager did what the regional VP requested, he was on his way to a big promotion. All of a sudden the proverbial shit hit the fan.

An investigation uncovered that the regional VP was instructing the sales manager he was grooming to double-count sales, using another sales organization to process his team's orders. This led the company to pay double the sales compensation for the same product sale. This was clearly a code of conduct violation with grounds for firing. The sales manager clearly knew of his unethical behavior, but he let his aspirations fog his judgment.

With this one act, all of his hard work to climb the corporate ladder was erased. The regional VP's more-than-30-year career was tarnished as he took down this sales manager with him. Both were fired, leaving behind burned bridges and tainted reputations.

Years of hard work can be incurably damaged with one lapse in integrity. There are countless examples of this, from former Penn State football coach Joe Paterno's cover-up of a man's sexual abuse of children to Tiger Woods's infidelity. Gaps in integrity don't always have to be grand plans to circumvent the rules. They often start small, but lead to bigger **DOPE** behavior after people realize they can get away with it (at first).

Building integrity is difficult, takes time, and is core to the reputation that others will perpetuate about you. Integrity is needed to gain others' trust in you and your abilities, and if your integrity is pliable then it will destroy trust and derail your career.

Much of the commentary thus far has focused on the negatives of not showing integrity, but it's important to note that having integrity has many benefits. Integrity solidifies your legacy and opens many doors for **STAR**s to gain rich career experiences.

Building integrity involves rolling up your sleeves and consistently doing unglamorous (but important) things. You create a strong sense that you are a young leader with integrity by doing the following:

★ Admit when you don't know something, then learn what you need to know.

★ Follow through on your commitments.

★ Take ownership of your work.

★ Stand up for what you believe is right, even when it's unpopular.

★ Take responsibility for your failures.

Integrity is the glue that holds your career together and keeps your reputation intact. Don't be the **DOPE** by risking your integrity for a short-term gain. Building a strong sense of integrity through time will lead to many new opportunities.

Three things cannot be long hidden: the sun, the moon, and the truth.

—Buddha

The STAR vs. the DOPE

The DOPE… Will compromise rules and beliefs to succeed. He starts small and then allows the line between right and wrong to become blurry.

The STAR… Gives up an easy win to maintain her integrity. She has clear guiding principles and fights for what she thinks is right.

CHAPTER 25

Let Others Help You
Be the *STAR*:
Be Coachable

What to Expect: We have all had coaches and teachers in our lives. They call us out on our issues and challenge us to be better. This chapter looks into how the many forms of "coaches" and how they are important.

When the student is ready, the teacher will appear.
—Buddhist proverb

Once the person commits to being coached, s/he begins to experience a different, more hopeful world as his or her perceptions evolve.
—John G. Agnos

She was a great candidate. Definitely someone I was going to pass along to the final round. Smart and savvy with a great set of previous experience, she had just what we wanted in a candidate. I was getting ready to send an e-mail with my recommendation that she have a final-round interview when an e-mail appeared in my inbox from the candidate.

The note started off fine. She thanked me for my time, complimented my experience, and offered a recap of the reasons she would be perfect for the position we were hiring for. Then—BOOM—she crashed and burned. At the end of the note, she mentioned that I should expect an e-mail momentarily with a $5 Starbucks gift card. The first thought that popped into my head was that she was bribing me. Maybe she thought that this gift would "seal the deal" and ensure her a final-round interview. But it was a big mistake. The note was totally impersonal. I hate coffee.

My disbelief and disappointment soon took a turn as I remembered something that happened to me a few months prior. It was a situation in which my coachability saved me from a big mistake. I applied for a promotion and was about to have the first round of interviews with the hiring manager. I had brought an updated version of my resume and had prepared for a discussion about my qualifications. It had been a few years since I had interviewed for a job, so I was a bit rusty, but I still thought I was ready.

As I sat down, the hiring manager embarked down one of the two typical starting points in an interview. "Take me through your resume," he said (the other starting point being "Tell me about yourself."). About 30 seconds into my somewhat bumbling answer he stopped me. "Start over again. Be more crisp," he advised. So I started again. This time, about 15 seconds later he stopped me again. "No, no, no. In this job you will be communicating with top executives at AT&T and it is important that you are direct and to the point." Instead of giving up or having the somewhat typical "chip on my shoulder" response, I took his instructions as an opportunity to learn.

The hiring manager began to offer me tips on how to explain my personal experience in a concise manner. I flipped over my resume and began taking notes on exactly what he said. At the same time, though, I was pretty stunned. In the past, friends had coached me (and I had coached others) before an interview on how to talk with a certain hiring manager, yet I had never experienced the hiring manager directly giving me tips on how to have a better interview with him.

In the next round of interviews, I showed him how his advice had really improved my communication ability. I was concise and communicated clearly and in a structured manner. I ended up getting the promotion. I imagine that one of the big reasons I got the job was because I took the hiring manager's coaching and eagerly implemented it.

Quick Tip

Don't be the scapegoat. Some bosses like to have favorites—and also scapegoats who get harsher feedback and are cut less slack. Generally the scapegoat is someone who does not know how to talk to the boss or has not improved when given constructive feedback. Adapt to coaching from your boss.

Remembering this experience, I decided I would give my candidate a chance as well. In response to her e-mail, I offered some coaching tips on how to write a solid interview follow-up thank-you note, keying in on how her gift could be construed as a bribe. Then I awaited her response. I was going to pin my final decision on how coachable she was. Her response was prompt, thanking me for my feedback and illustrating that she had learned a valuable lesson that she would keep in mind going forward. I passed her on to the final round and she accepted a full-time offer with the company. Through the rest of the interview and decision-making process she kept me up to date, further referencing her appreciation for the coaching I gave her.

So much about being the *STAR* is about the ability to learn. Taking lessons from every situation (Chapter 9) and being a fast learner (Chapter 6) are important foundational characteristics, but your coachability really reveals your willingness to learn *in action*.

We have all had a coach at some point in our lives, from organized sports to an organization like Girl Scouts. I think we all can agree that coaches can be very helpful in getting us to perform at our best. Everyone needs a coach. Even Tiger Woods, one of the best golfers of all time, still has a coach to help him perfect his swing. No matter how self-aware we are, there are certain things that we cannot see in ourselves. We need others to help us identify our gaps and offer suggestions for improvement.

*DOPE*s let ego get in the way of the opportunity to improve. They may discount the source and downplay the validity of any statement because it is critical of them. Instead, the *STAR* realizes that she can find coaches everywhere, in both large and small ways.

Quick Tip

Ask about expectations up-front from your boss and other people you work with; it will let you know what they want from you, and it will also make it easier for them to give you coaching and feedback.

Potential coaches are all around us. A coach can be a mentor, your boss, a peer, or even someone who works for you.

I vividly recall how the top salesperson on one of my previous teams taught me that achieving higher performance is a team effort. When I took a regional sales manager role, I focused on making the top salespeople more successful, not paying much attention to the others. Soon our team fell behind the other teams.

Then my top salesperson took matters into his own hands. He began coaching his peers and ensuring everyone did well. Results began to pick up. I saw this and made it my mission to ensure that everyone on my team met quota. This led to a three-year period when every single person who worked for me was over 100 percent of their annual target. If I had stifled my employee's initiative and didn't take the improved results as a lesson that I perpetuated, we never would have accomplished what we did.

Being open to feedback from all angles is the central concept of effective coachability. Unlikely sources can provide you with some of the best lessons. Being coachable isn't a reactive trait. Someone who is coachable actively hunts for best practices and lessons in her experience, and also is able to take a step back and observe (a form of being coached).

In a previous role, I worked very closely with another direct report to my VP, a recently promoted director who had been a part in the leadership program I was in. He was not a talkative person, but for some reason when he talked, people listened. I began to study his communication skills and then actively approached him to discuss possible lessons I could glean from him. This led to practical advice that I still use today.

*STAR*s understand what the coaching process must involve. The **STAR** actively listens to constructive feedback, thanks the feedback provider for his or her insights, internalizes the message that was being communicated, and then finally takes more educated action going forward. (Remember, "To know and not to do is not to know.")

Remember that each step in this process is crucial, from being willing to listen to coaching to changing your behavior because of it. When a mentor coaches you and sees that you implement his teaching, he will be motivated by your improvements and will often continue to put time and energy into making you better.

Actively listen when someone is coaching you, and constantly seek out coaches who can help you improve and fast-track your career. My coachability has gotten me jobs, earned me additional responsibilities, opened me up to unique experiences, and inspired others to believe in me.

People only see what they are prepared to see.
—Ralph Waldo Emerson

The STAR vs. the DOPE

The DOPE... Doesn't find value in constructive feedback and allows his ego to prevent himself from improving.

The STAR... Knows that a mentor can appear from anywhere. She listens and adapts according to good advice.

CHAPTER 26

It's Never too Early to Pay It Forward:
The Importance of Giving Back

What to Expect: Although it is natural to get wrapped up in all the things going on in your life, it is important to dedicate time and effort to helping others. This chapter discusses why giving back is a critical part of being the **STAR**.

Successful people are always looking for opportunities to help others. Unsuccessful people are always asking "What's in it for me?"
—Brian Tracy

He who gives when he is asked has waited too long.
—*Sunshine Magazine*

My eyes lit up as I looked down at my newest treasure.

I must be special! For the first time I actually got someone's business card! I didn't know whether to frame it or have my mom put it on the refrigerator to show it off.

No, this wasn't following a networking event I attended recently. I was in eighth grade and it was the last day of our Junior Achievement program. A manager from Visa had come into our classroom to teach us about business throughout the previous couple of months, and that day we were "graduating." Besides getting a certificate for participating in the program (another example of something that helped create the millennial sense of entitlement), I received my first business card ever. Handing it out meant nothing to the manager from Visa, but it sure meant a whole lot to me. It was one of the first glimpses I had into what the working world was really like.

Giving back, the way the Visa manager did for me, makes an impact. Whether it is a few dollars or a few hours of your time, it really matters to those in need. But it's easy to put off focusing on helping others. After all, we are still figuring out our own lives; how can we be expected to help others when *we* have no clue? This sentiment is true of almost any generation, but is particularly true of our generation. With such an intense focus on ourselves (we have been called the "Me Generation"), intensified by our parents, it can be hard for us to remember to dedicate time and energy to others.

I am not saying that we are completely selfish as young people. On the contrary, I think that many of us have a heightened social consciousness, a deeply rooted desire to help those less fortunate than ourselves. I am only asserting that with how crazy our lives are, the concept of "giving back" is often one of the first things to go by the wayside when we get busy.

Quick Tip

Small things help. You don't have to make a huge time commitment by taking on a large role within an organization to truly give back. Start by doing one thing a month that helps others less fortunate. Even the little things count.

Instead of laying out an argument about the effect giving back can have on others, I would like to focus on another reason why we should give back (I will leave to the multitude of evidence out there the explanations of why you donating your time, effort, and money helps others): Focus on helping others because it teaches us, not because it makes us feel good. Giving back often comes in the form of teaching others.

According to William Glasser, "We learn: 10 percent of what we read; 20 percent of what we hear; 30 percent of what we both see and hear; 50 percent of what we discussed with others; 80 percent of what we experience personally; 95 percent of what we teach to someone else." I agree wholeheartedly with this statement because of personal experience. I see the concept of *teaching* being a part of the notion of *helping* others. One of the main reasons I gained such a solid understanding of leadership was not just that I took on leadership positions but that I taught a course on leadership for four semesters when I was in college. When you have to teach someone something it makes you prepare more and gives you a deeper understanding of it. The **STAR** knows that going through the process of preparing to teach others is the best way to get a full understanding of a topic—you have to be ready for any question asked and you don't want to look like an idiot in front of your student.

Why else is giving back an important part of being the **STAR**?

Helping others can help you professionally. Not only does it help your personal brand (think about how companies donate millions of dollars and fund vast social campaigns not only to support causes they believe in, but also to look good to their customers), but it also expands your network. Allowing others to see you within the constructs of a "giving" situation takes off some of the pressure of a relationship that would otherwise be strictly business. A few years ago I joined an amazing organization called the Full Circle Fund, which focuses on giving grants and pro-bono operational and strategic consulting to social entrepreneurs. I am inspired by the work these social entrepreneurs do and I believe in the causes they fight for—and I have also developed many relationships applicable to my current job.

Giving back also brings variety to our lives. It facilitates a better work/life balance. It allows us to focus on things outside of our work and family lives. It can also inspire us and provide us with a stronger sense of fulfillment, because we are not just taking, but also giving.

Opportunities to help others come in all shapes and sizes. Helping others is not just working with kids or giving to the underprivileged. You can give back by being a mentor to someone who has less experience than you. Ultimately the most important part of this concept is the mindset behind giving back. *STAR*s make it about others.

There are many ways to effectively give back. Everything from helping a peer with reviewing something he is about to turn in to his boss, to offering advice to someone in a tough situation, to joining a community organization are all forms of giving back. *STAR*s who have a giving mindset find opportunities everywhere to give to others.

Quick Tip

Give back to yourself: Take a vacation. Many young professionals don't take time off work. Take the time you have earned and disconnect from work to reenergize. Don't check work e-mail while you are taking time off. I usually travel internationally so that I can fully disconnect from work.

One of the best ways to give back is finding something that you are passionate about and identifying ways to positively affect that area. For example, I am passionate about education. This passion has driven me to be a big brother for the Big Brothers Big Sisters organization, become a classroom volunteer for Junior Achievement of America, and focus on education within the Full Circle Fund.

Be creative about how you choose to give back. It isn't just about donating money or volunteering for a large nonprofit organization. For example, I wanted to give back to my godmother, who has been fighting for equality causes for more than 50 years. As a 75th birthday gift, I created the Jill Wakeman Foundation for Equality, and launched a giving campaign that received a great deal of press and now will serve as a way to make her legacy live on. I saw an opportunity to give back to someone who had given so much to me (and others).

Next, use your resources and talents to increase the impact of your giving. For example, I have been able to leverage my business strategy, sales and operations skills, and experience to help teams of social entrepreneurs through being a mentor for teams competing in the Global Social Venture Competition.

Finally, remember that it is not about the magnitude of how you give back. You don't have to decide to quit your job and work full-time in the nonprofit space in order to make a solid impact. Small things (like giving a business card to a kid) can make a big difference to those you are helping.

Don't wait until you retire, become an executive, or get that next promotion to give back. Giving back can be as simple as being a mentor, offering advice to someone in need, or donating a few dollars and a couple of hours to support a cause you are passionate about. It's never too early to start.

Great opportunities to help others seldom come, but small ones surround us every day.
—Sally Koch

We make a living by what we get, but we make a life by what we give.
—Sir Winston Churchill

The STAR vs. the DOPE

The DOPE… Waits until he is well on his way to accomplishing his goals before helping others.

The STAR… Puts the goal of giving above the opportunity to be in the limelight. She understands that giving back helps not only those she is serving but herself as well.

CHAPTER 27

The Determining Factor of Success in Your Career: Getting Results

What to Expect: This chapter ties together many of the characteristics of **STAR**s that have been discussed throughout the book and explains why even when someone masters all of them she will still end up being the **DOPE** if she can't deliver results.

I have long since come to believe that people never mean half of what they say, and that it is best to disregard their talk and judge only their actions.

—Dorothy Day, *The Long Loneliness*

Well done is better than well said.

—Benjamin Franklin

189

Here is where everything comes together.

All of the attributes we have discussed and the "house" that you have built manifest themselves in the results that you generate.

Whereas being well-liked is nice, your career success is measured by what you are able to accomplish. Often the true determination of whether you are the *DOPE* or the *STAR* hinges on the results you produce.

While managing an operations team I interviewed a young professional for an open position. He was very impressive. From the folder he put his resume in to the way he communicated, everything came across very professionally. He was extremely likeable and had a good track record in previous jobs. He ended up going to work for a peer of mine and then through a reorganization was put on my team. It became apparent within only a matter of days that there was no substance behind his great first impression. He exuded many of the attributes discussed, from patience to creativity to having a positive attitude, but he didn't get results.

When coaching him, he would say that he understood how to be successful at his job. But there was no follow-through. I put him on a performance improvement plan, and eventually he was fired.

Results are about substance.

How you accomplish results is also important. Being the best but burning bridges all along the way is not the best strategy. My speech-plagiarizing "friend" referenced earlier was a successful and impressive person, but as you got to know him, it became apparent that he was always looking out for himself (the *DOPE* thing to do). He seemed to see people for how they could help him. He was willing to damage a relationship to get what he wanted. This strategy will eventually catch up with you and does not lead to sustainable success. You can find examples of people who successfully make their way to the top in a destructive manner, but there are many more examples of people who crash and burn with this strategy.

A while ago I was talking with a group of friends and the topic of who is the best team sports athlete came up. In response, I didn't choose Michael Jordan. I felt the answer lies in identifying the core purpose of playing a sport. When it comes to team sports, what is the goal? To win championships. And when it comes to winning championships there was no one better than Bill Russell. In 17 years of playing basketball, from college to the pros, Bill Russell won 13 championships. He won two NCAA championships and 11 championships in 13 years as a Boston Celtic in the 1950s and '60s. No one can even come close to this. Moreover, he accomplished all of this without a bunch of flash. He based his success on principles.

The thing that struck me about Bill Russell is how cerebral he is about the game of basketball. In his book, *Russell Rules*, he discussed the importance of being a leader on the team, which sometimes meant passing the ball even when he really wanted to score. He also noted how many of the attributes discussed in this book can lead to success, from decision-making skills to integrity to the importance of hard work. All of these center on driving results and attaining goals.

Quick Tip

Prep time. Use Sunday night to prepare for the week. Just as in the scavenger hunt example referenced earlier, it is a good idea to take a step back to plan. Pre-plan your week to focus on what you want to accomplish. This will give you a leg up over those who wait until Monday morning to re-engage.

Driving results is about follow-through. As young and energetic leaders we are full of creative ideas, and are constantly looking for ways to do things better and improve the organizations we are a part of. Yet I have seen many times when our peers will introduce a great idea, start working on it, and then lose steam, either because of a shift in interest or because an obstacle arises.

Following through to get results is about resiliency. It's about being proactive and being flexible when change occurs, and never giving up.

Getting results is important, but the question surfaces: _How can we get results?_ There are a number of tactics to use. Set goals to know what end result toward which you want to drive. Without knowing where point B is, it is nearly impossible to get to where you want to go. Tie your goals in with those of your boss and your organization and there will be a much higher likelihood of success and positive results.

Next, it is important to know your metrics. Understand how you are being judged. In sales, measuring results is easy; you either met your quota or you didn't. In other roles it is more difficult to understand whether you are doing a good job or not. Understand how you are being measured and what success looks like for the job you are in.

Then, break down the large goal you want to attain into actions you can take to get there. Improve on the items you can control and work within the parameters of those you can't. Planning is an important part of getting results. If you blindly go out and do your job, you are squandering your opportunities (a very **DOPE** thing to do).

Aligning your time with the results you want to achieve is key as well. This is closely followed by monitoring your progress so you know how close you are to the results you want. I recently heard Sandra Kurtzig speak at a technology conference I attended for work. She was one of the first successful female entrepreneurs in the Silicon Valley, starting the Ask Group in 1972. When presenting, she said that successful people "don't chase 'shiny objects.'" Don't get distracted by things that hinder you from getting results. Then have the discipline to follow through.

Quick Tip

Tell people your age—after you achieve great results. It is best to keep your young age secret from your coworkers. When you act professionally they will assume you are older. After you have accomplished significant results, then share your age.

Coworkers will be incredibly impressed instead of resentful, which they often are if they find out you are young early on in your relationship with them.

Getting results is also about consistency. The main difference between a professional baseball player and a minor league player is not skill; the difference is consistency. A professional has to be able to get hits and make plays 164 games a season. Our careers are not about completing one project and then riding off into the sunset. It is about stringing together results from many different positions, ensuring they build on each other.

When working toward getting results, focus on the job at hand, not on creating hype and flash. Many people have never heard of Sam Wyly. Without all the pomp and circumstance he built six different billion-dollar businesses in the last 60 years, going up against and beating many market-leading companies in the process. In the end, it is about what you did, not the smoke and mirrors you created to make yourself look good.

While driving results, make sure that you balance *patience* with *taking action*. Time is paramount. Sometimes you have to wait for certain things to take place to achieve a result. Other times you need to move quickly. **STAR**s understand this and are able to determine which situations require action and which require patience.

Once you do achieve results, though, don't let it go to your head. **DOPE**s begin to let their ego and sense of entitlement take over.

So are you driving results? The best way to find out is by looking at your resume. If your results are not where you want them to be, go out and do something about it.

Vision without execution is a hallucination.
—Einstein

Explore Online

Career Exterior blueprint: On TheSparkSource. com, go to the Resources page to find a diagram and summary of the attributes that are visible to those you work with.

The STAR vs. the DOPE

The DOPE... Thinks that doing his job will lead to bonuses, raises, and promotions.

The STAR... Understands that consistently delivering results, no matter the job or the challenges she faces, will lead to a successful career.

Attributes 18 Through 25 of the STAR Young Professional

The STAR vs. the DOPE

*18. The **DOPE**...* Expects others to understand what he communicates.
*The **STAR**...* Takes ownership of her communication. She ensures others understand what she communicates by adapting to her audience and following up.

*19. The **DOPE**...* Gets caught up in the emotion or frustration of a bad situation, and lets his negativity show.
*The **STAR**...* Understands that her attitude affects her quality of work and the way other people view her. She keeps an open mind, looking for new options and positives in the face of adversity.

*20. The **DOPE**...* Expects others to help him succeed and rise to the top without helping them first.
*The **STAR**...* Sees that people will be inspired to help her if she finds a way to help them first, without expecting anything in return.

*21. The **DOPE**...* Believes there is no crossover between work life and social life.
*The **STAR**...* Understands that people are always watching and that even one slip-up can damage a painstakingly built reputation.

22. *The* **DOPE**… Will compromise rules and beliefs to
succeed. He starts small and then allows the line
between right and wrong to become blurry.
The **STAR**… Gives up an easy win to maintain her
integrity. She has clear guiding principles and fights
for what she thinks is right.

23. *The* **DOPE**… Doesn't find value in constructive
feedback and allows his ego to prevent himself from
improving.
The **STAR**… Knows that a mentor can appear from
anywhere. She listens and adapts according to good
advice.

24. *The* **DOPE**… Waits until he is well on his way to accomplishing his goals before helping others.
The **STAR**… Puts the goal of giving above the opportunity to be in the limelight. She understands that
giving back helps not only those she is serving but
herself as well.

25. *The* **DOPE**… Thinks that doing his job will lead to
bonuses, raises, and promotions.
The **STAR**… Understands that consistently delivering
results, no matter the job or the challenges she faces,
will lead to a successful career.

PART V

Bringing It All Together

In this final section, you will explore how to apply the concepts and attributes discussed throughout the book. You will learn to put together and implement your career blueprint to lead you down the path to being a *STAR*.

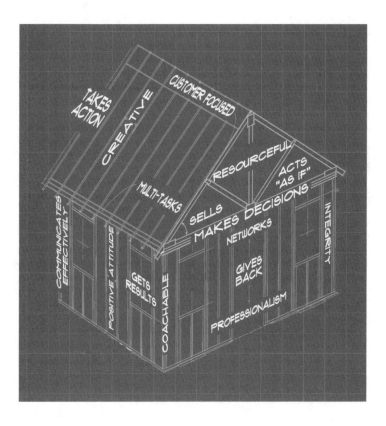

CHAPTER 28

Crafting Your Own
STAR Mindset

What to Expect: Now that you have learned all the attributes of the **STAR**, it's time to build your own house, from foundation to frame to exterior. This chapter helps you create a career blueprint that develops the 25 attributes of the **STAR**.

Write your goals in concrete and your plans in sand.
—Anonymous

Everyone thinks of changing the world, but no one thinks of changing himself.
—Leo Nikolaevich Tolstoy

Explore Online

Go to TheSparkSource.com and take the *STAR* post-assessment on the Young Professional's Guide Resources page. This will provide you with insights into attributes you excel in and others that need improvement.

Now that you have read about all 25 of the attributes that make young professionals successful, the next step is to create your own career blueprint.

When building a house, architects use blueprints to guide the contractors and builders on what to do to construct the house. These blueprints include details on all the materials to be used and all the measurements to be followed.

Your career blueprint takes the attributes that are strengths and those that are weaknesses and lays out a design for improvement from the online assessment. Use the Career Blueprint template from TheSparkSource.com to design a plan for how you are going to improve on the attributes you rated as those of a *DOPE* and transform your *STAR* attributes into your professional brand. It is our natural tendency to focus on weaknesses that prevent us from being successful. Although it's useful to be aware of what you are not good at, you should focus primarily on transforming what you *are* good at into attributes you are known and revered for, forming your brand. Be mindful of where you fell into the *DOPE* category and build a plan to ensure these traits don't end up turning into career-limiting flaws.

Your personal brand consists of the top two or three *STAR* attributes. These are the characteristics on which you ranked highest that, with development, you can become known for. As you actualize these traits, they will pave the way to career opportunities and become reasons why people want you in their organizations.

As you progress through your career, you will face many important decisions: go the corporate or entrepreneurial route? Take the management or individual contributor track? Build a broad set of experiences or deep expertise? Relocate for a big promotion or stay in your current geographic area? Odds are we will have to answer some, if not all of these questions at some point in our careers. The thought of having to make life-changing decisions can be daunting, but it's important to remember that there is no *right* answer. You can make a decision that leads down one path or a decision that takes you down another and still end up at the same end result. As long as you embody the traits of the **STAR**, you will be successful in whatever path you take.

After solidifying your **DOPE**, **STAR**, and personal brand traits and building a plan for improvements, expand the scope of your blueprint to look at your entire career. In building a comprehensive career blueprint, it's important to answer questions like:

* ✯ What is the overall career mission and vision you want to attain? (A heavy question to start with, I know.)

* ✯ What goals do you want to accomplish in your career (three years from now, five years from now, and 20 years from now)? Make these SMART goals.

* ✯ What experiences do you need in order to attain specific goals and reach your ultimate career vision?

* ✯ What are some alternatives you would be happy with if things don't go your way?

* ✯ What are the steps associated with reaching your goal?

* ✯ How are you going to monitor your progress and celebrate small successes?

* ✯ How can the branding and competitive advantages you discovered in your **STAR** assessment be leveraged to move you closer to your goal?

* ✯ Who can help you reach your goals?

Use the insights from your answers to fill out the rest of your Career Blueprint template. When answering these kinds of questions, make sure that your answers are realistic and practical with specific actions outlined; the more abstract, the harder to enact.

Quick Tip

Talk about your career goals. Never turn down an opportunity to chat with someone about his future either; you never know when you will need the returned favor.

Next, prioritize each of your goals and the steps you must take to attain them. You won't have enough bandwidth to accomplish everything at once, and you must be patient in the process. Moreover, your priorities will help you evaluate opportunities that come your way. Prioritizing your goals (along with leveraging your intuition, past experiences, and advice from others) is the best way to accurately and effectively decide whether an opportunity is right for you.

The main reason it is important to put together your career blueprint is to know what you are aiming for. Identifying what you want will clarify the next steps you should be taking. Remember that as a **STAR** you have to be flexible. Just because you set a goal and career vision now does not mean you have to commit to it for the next 40 years. Circumstances change. Your interests change. Your career plan should change as well. Establish a list of both career and five-year goals that you update once a year (both found on your Career Blueprint template). Leveraging this simple format goes a long way in aligning my actions and priorities with my goals and ultimate career vision.

Although there will be times when you do not feel in control, remember that you are still the author of your career. You get to decide how each of the chapters is written.

Do not let what you cannot do interfere with what you can do.
—John Wooden, *They Call Me Coach*

Explore Online

Go to TheSparkSource.com and look under Resources to find your Career Blueprint templates.

The STAR vs. the DOPE

The **DOPE**... Looks to eliminate all his weaknesses before improving his strengths. He doesn't create success plans or goals, and lets his career own him instead of taking ownership of his career. The **STAR**... Leverages strengths to create a strong brand, continually building on them to be even better while eliminating career derailers. She builds a blueprint for career success.

CHAPTER 29

Putting Your *STAR* Mindset Into Action

What to Expect: Putting together a comprehensive career blueprint and development plan is important but is ultimately worthless without implementation. This chapter shows you how to put your plan and everything learned in this book into action.

Watch your thoughts for they become words. Watch your words for they become actions. Watch your actions for they become habits. Watch your habits, for they become your character. And watch your character, for it becomes your destiny! What we think we become.

—Margaret Thatcher, from the film *The Iron Lady*

Do a little more each day than you think you possibly can.

—Lowell Thomas

Now that you took the time to build your career blueprint, the next step is to implement your plan. As Albert Einstein said, "Vision without execution is a hallucination." It's great to talk about all these important career-related topics, but it's worthless unless you actually *do* something about it. This is the stage in the development process where work actually gets done. This is where your house is built and where your career takes shape.

The following are important considerations that will help you be successful at becoming the **STAR** and implementing your career blueprint.

* **Be flexible with follow-through.** One of the most important things **STAR**s master when implementing their career plans is to stay true to their career blueprint while simultaneously being agile in how to get to their goal. Realize that the path to your goals will often be full of unexpected changes, and know that it is acceptable to adapt your goals as your life changes.

* **Listen.** Listening is one of the most important parts of communicating. In the article "Are You Listening to Your Life," Parker Palmer writes, "Vocation, I've learned, doesn't come from willfulness. It comes from listening.... I must listen for what my life wants to do with me.... If we can learn to read our own responses, we'll receive the guidance we need to live more authentic lives."[1] Listen for the right opportunities that will bring you closer to your goals.

* **Take risks and get experience.** Implementing your career blueprint involves risk. Make sure to take advantage of the fact that you are younger and have fewer commitments than when you get older (mortgages, kids, bills, and so on). When starting my mobile application company, I originally had two partners, but when it came time to commit more time and money to the project, one partner was unable to continue because of his existing financial and time commitments. His opportunity to fail forward fast had come and gone. One of the best ways to successfully achieve your

career goals is to get experience. Even if the situation is not perfect, you can still derive great lessons. These experiences also help you understand when good and bad opportunities come along.

✯ **Take baby steps.** Implementing your career blueprint is not about making huge life changes. What's more important are small, consistent steps toward your goals. These often-overlooked small steps will have a far greater effect on whether you will have a successful career.

✯ **Do the dirty work.** Be willing to roll up your sleeves. Going through each of the steps to reach your career goals will involve *less-than-glamorous* experiences. These experiences often have a great impact on the future leader you become.

✯ **Be engaged in your own career.** Don't always be looking ahead or analyzing things you did in the past. Be present in the here and now. Mistakes are made and *STAR*s are built in the present moment. If you are not paying attention to your actions and how they affect attaining what you outlined in your career blueprint, then you will most likely fail. It's hard to monitor your progress with the plan if you're not paying attention.

✯ **Leverage momentum in your favor.** Positive inertia can be a great thing. Once you build a strong reputation and produce great results, better opportunities will come your way. Once you start to head down the path toward reaching your career goals, leverage great things that happen to you. At the same time, though, be mindful of negative momentum. One *DOPE* move can lead to a string of mistakes.

✯ **Balance thinking and doing.** The *STAR* takes action. Yet successfully implementing these principles involves thinking through not only the development of your *STAR* plan but also the best ways to execute your plan.

✯ **Take time to reflect.** Setting time aside to examine whether your career is on track can be difficult, if not impossible.

If you don't set time aside you won't do it. Your work and personal life will be like your e-mail inbox: continually piling up with stuff to do. Just as with e-mail, there is a lot of spam and a whole bunch of busywork with a few important things mixed in. It is important to set time aside to reflect on the things you have done well, the areas where you are struggling, and the progress you have made in reaching your career goals. This reflection time should examine your performance, emotions, general fulfillment, and **STAR** trait development. As Ralph Waldo Emerson said, "The field cannot well be seen from within the field." Remember to take a step back.

★ **Challenge yourself.** Be willing to enter into situations in which you are over your head. Get out of your comfort zone. How will you know what your limitations are until you put them to the test?

★ **Be okay with making mistakes.** Failure happens and is one of the best ways to learn important lessons that will help you later in your career. If you go in with the mindset that you will either get closer to reaching your goals by succeeding or uncovering a way *not* to do things (in other words, failing), then any experience is valuable.

★ **Be comfortable with your unique plan.** Although it is natural for the career paths others take to affect the way you look at your own career path, understand that your path is unique and specific to you. Don't constantly change your goals to match a model you saw that worked one time for one person. Have confidence that with patience, you will reach the goals you want.

And finally, the most important step in successfully implementing your career blueprint: **successfully leverage mentorship.** This is by far the most effective way to reach your career goals, although it is probably one of the most underutilized. When young professionals whom I have managed want to talk to me about how to get promoted and attain career goals, I always accept their offer. When considering being a mentor I ask them to set up a meeting with me to talk about their career plan in more detail. I also give them a quick assignment: organize their thoughts and write out their career goals. Most never even schedule the follow-up meeting, squandering an opportunity.

Mentoring often gets pushed off because it is not given high priority. Meetings with my AT&T mentor often have to be rescheduled three or four times because of prior commitments my mentor has. It's important not to give up, especially because the best mentors are incredibly busy. You have to set time aside for mentorship and take the lead in your mentoring relationships. It is the job of the mentee to engage the mentor.

Mentoring opens doors for you that normally would not be open. Mentors can help you network and make connections, but mainly mentors free you from making many of the mistakes they made. As Sam Levenson proclaims, "You must learn from the mistakes of others. You can't possibly live long enough to make them all yourself." The **STAR** knows this and leverages mentors to keep from making unnecessary mistakes.

Don't be afraid to ask mentors the tough questions, because they have answers. Mentors have already been there. They have faced adversity and failed, then persevered to be successful. In our home-building metaphor, mentors know the materials to use and the techniques to leverage in order to build a strong house (a strong career).

Quick Tip

Connect with your mentor. Find a mentor you connect with personally first, and then ensure he or she also aligns with your professional goals.

Just as with coaching, mentoring comes in many forms.

Traditionally, mentors are thought only to be very experienced executives or accomplished people in the position you aspire to reach. They have amazing wisdom, but it often comes at the expense of understanding what life is like for people our age. This flavor of mentor often cannot relate as well to the challenges we have and therefore might find it hard to really help you with your difficult career issues. With the long passing of time, they either forget or misconstrue the details. Whereas many traditional mentors understand how they made their way to the top of their field, these methods may be obsolete as markets and strategies change.

Also, when selecting mentors, young professionals often take too wide of a scope. A mentor doesn't only have to help you with your career at a macro level; mentors can help you with little steps along the way. These situations are perfect for what I call *mini-mentors*. Mini-mentors help you learn one aspect of a new job or provide specific details on how to be successful in a specific situation. Mini-mentors are very niche. At any given time, you could have dozens of mini-mentors who help you specifically with one aspect of your job or overall professional life.

You also benefit from mentoring others. Helping those younger or less experienced than you helps you better understand what you have done to be successful in your career thus far. This helps you continue doing the good things and reminds you of the mistakes you never want to make again.

Quick Tip

Tell people about yours goals. Establishing a goal is just the beginning. When you write down your goals and look at them from time to time you will become more committed to them, but ultimate commitment comes when you tell other people about your goals. Because you know that they will follow up with you to see if you have accomplished your goals, there is a higher likelihood you will do what is necessary to meet that goal and follow through on your verbal commitment.

Finally, there is peer mentoring. Peer mentoring is probably the most overlooked form of mentoring. Peer mentoring occurs in many other areas of our lives but often not in our careers, so we don't notice it in action. If you look back on your life, you will find that you have certainly experienced peer mentoring: If you have a younger sibling, odds are you have mentored them on anything from how to get away with disobeying your parents to how to act around someone you want to date. If you have older siblings, odds are they have mentored you. Even if you are an only child you most likely learned a lot from an older cousin or friend. You also probably have used Yelp before; this is a form of peer mentoring for restaurants and other local businesses, because you are asking your peer patrons for advice instead of consulting a critic's official review.

Peer mentoring works because our peers understand us. As millennials we know what it's like to be from our generation and face similar issues. Peers can be creative and often have relatable experience fresh in their minds, because oftentimes it recently happened to them.

In building a mentoring plan, develop a blended plan that involves each of these types of mentors. And remember that although you can choose a mentor, mentors also choose you. As mentioned, the people from whom you could learn the most are incredibly busy and are often very selective about whom they chose to mentor. Be bold enough to ask for their help but be patient when building mentoring relationships and always show your appreciation for the advice that is given to you. It is up to you to follow up and keep the relationship going.

Many things will contribute to you attaining your career goals, but identifying and leveraging mentors to help guide you is by far the most effective tool to help implement your strategy.

You are the person who has to decide. Whether you'll do it or toss it aside; You are the person who makes up your mind. Whether you'll lead or will linger behind. Whether you'll try for the goal that's afar. Or just be contented to stay where you are.

—Edgar A. Guest

Explore Online

One of the main features on TheSparkSource.com is a community for young professionals to offer each other peer mentorship in a safe and anonymous environment. You can post career-related questions and get advice back, and you have the ability to rate the advice others give you. Feel free to give your own advice, too.

The STAR vs. the DOPE

The DOPE… Develops a great plan to build a strong house (career) and then makes excuses to keep him from successfully implementing it, thinking that making the plan is enough.

The STAR… Enacts a solid plan and monitors progress as she builds her career, graciously leveraging mentors to ensure her success.

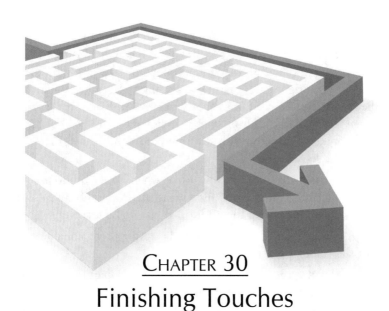

CHAPTER 30
Finishing Touches

Excellence is not a destination; it is a continuous journey that never ends.

—Brian Tracy

A good example has twice the value of good advice.

—Unknown

Twenty years from now you will be more disappointed by the things that you didn't do than by the ones you did do. So throw off the bowlines. Sail away from the safe harbor. Catch the trade winds in your sails. Explore. Dream. Discover.

—Mark Twain

It was my last day on the job; I was moving on to a new position within AT&T. As I packed up my box of belongings at my desk, I looked over at the giant, blown-up, framed picture of my ID badge that my team signed and gave me as a going-away present. I gazed at the messages from each of my coworkers, wishing me well, sharing things they had learned from me, and reliving the fun experiences we had together. I knew that I had learned more from them than they ever could have learned from me.

I was excited and optimistic, just as when I walked into my first performance review. But this time I was smarter. I had made some mistakes, but because of them I learned how to be successful.

As we conclude the first book of the Young Professional's Series, let's take a look back at what we learned.

We learned the 25 attributes that set **STAR**s apart from **DOPE**s. We investigated these key traits in the context of building a house: having a strong foundation (core personal characteristics), maintaining a sturdy frame and structure (the traits relating to *how* you do things), and the exterior of the house (the attributes that are visible to others and affect their perception of you).

We investigated how to create a career blueprint, to build these key traits and to ensure that you will be a **STAR** by detailing how to implement the plan you created.

As you continue through you career, remember:

* ✮ **Don't worry.** As Ryan Reynolds's character said in the movie *Van Wilder*, "Worrying is like a rocking chair. It gives you something to do but it doesn't get you anywhere." Don't stress about getting everything right all the time.

* ✮ **It's okay not to know.** So many questions arise in our professional lives and there are even more answers and possibilities to consider. Don't get overwhelmed. It is okay to admit that you don't have the right answer. **STAR**s adapt when change occurs.

* ✮ **Don't tie your identity and self-worth to a job.** There is more to you than your career. Many Americans tie so much

of who they are to their jobs (which is one of the reasons being unemployed is psychologically exhausting). Anytime someone asks "What do you do?" our first response is always to answer with what our job is. Realize that it is better to connect your self-worth with your family, friends, and the exciting experiences you have in your life.

⋆ **Be a life long learner.** *STAR*s are not only fast learners but are also continuous learners. The moment you stop gaining knowledge is the moment you start losing it. Life long learners are constantly able to reinvent themselves and realize that the process of learning never stops.

⋆ **Enjoy the ride.** Yes, I know this is clichéd, but your career (similar to life) is about the journey and not just the end result. If you look ahead too much you will miss out on opportunities in the present. At the same time, if you don't look ahead at all you will trip and fall.

Besides emulating the 25 attributes of a successful young professional, remember the equation for success:

SUCCESS = PASSION × SKILL

How successful you are in your career is a product of the passion you have and the skills you leverage. As a multiplication equation, if either passion or skill is zero, then your success will also be zero. You will not be successful with skill alone. The secret lies in your passion. The trick of the equation is that even without skills, your passion will lead you to learn the skills you need to be successful.

Find your passion. It may not come right away and will most likely adapt in time, but you will find it.

Finally, be a leader. You don't need to have a fancy title or a big office to be a leader. True leadership is about taking ownership of your actions and always doing your best to use your unique talents in helping yourself and others reach goals.

As Chris Garner reminded me at that sales conference, you are not *just* anything. Realize how important you are to your company. You are not *just* an analyst. You are not *just* an associate. You are not *just* a mid-level manager.

You *are* a leader and a successful young professional with an exciting career ahead.

Notes

Chapter 4

1. Blanchard, Ken, and Mark Miller. "Great Leaders Grow: Becoming a Leader for Life." San Francisco: Berrett-Koehler Publishers, 2012. *http://greatleadersgrow.com.*

Chapter 10

1. Portillo, Ely. "New Poll Shows Many Think Millennials Aren't Hard Workers." *Chicago Tribune*, December 26, 2011. *http://articles.chicagotribune.com/2011-12-26/business/ ct-biz-1226-millennials-20111226_1_millennials-new-poll- older-workers.*

Chapter 12

1. Reicheld, Frederick F. *The Ultimate Question: Driving Good Profits and True Growth.* Cambridge, Mass.: Harvard Business School Press, 2006. *www.netpromotersystem.com/system-processes/measure-of-success.aspx.*

Chapter 20

1. Mehrabian, A. *Silent Messages: Implicit Communication of Emotions and Attitudes.* Belmont, Calif.: Wadsworth, 1981. *www.kaaj.com/psych/smorder.html.*

Chapter 29

1. Palmer, Parker J. *Let Your Life Speak: Listening for the Voice of Vocation.* San Francisco, Calif.: Jossey-Bass, 2000.

Index

About the Author

Aaron McDaniel is a corporate manager, entrepreneur, public speaker, and community leader. Aaron has held diverse management roles at AT&T, a Fortune 500 company, being one of the youngest to serve as regional vice president. Still in his 20s, Aaron is a serial entrepreneur and founder of multiple ventures, including Spark Source, a community focused on empowering young professionals to succeed in their careers. He is a graduate of UC Berkeley's Undergraduate Haas School of Business, where he instructed a highly rated student-led course on leadership.

Outside of his professional life, Aaron is an avid international traveler, having visited 33 countries to date. Passionate about giving back, Aaron founded the Jill Wakeman Foundation for Equality and is an active community volunteer in San Francisco, where he lives.